PENGUIN B

BREAKFAST WIT

Breakfast with Anglo

SIMON KELLY

PENGUIN BOOKS

PENGUIN BOOKS

Published by the Penguin Group
Penguin Books Ltd, 80 Strand, London WC2R ORL, England
Penguin Group (USA) Inc., 375 Hudson Street, New York, New York 10014, USA
Penguin Group (Canada), 90 Eglinton Avenue East, Suite 700, Toronto, Ontario, Canada M4P 2Y3
(a division of Pearson Penguin Canada Inc.)
Penguin Ireland, 25 St Stephen's Green, Dublin 2, Ireland (a division of Penguin Books Ltd)
Penguin Group (Australia), 250 Camberwell Road, Camberwell, Victoria 3124, Australia
(a division of Pearson Australia Group Pty Ltd)
Penguin Books India Pvt Ltd, 11 Community Centre, Panchsheel Park, New Delhi – 110 017, India
Penguin Group (NZ), 67 Apollo Drive, Rosedale, Auckland 0632, New Zealand
(a division of Pearson New Zealand Ltd)
Penguin Books (South Africa) (Pty) Ltd, 24 Sturdee Avenue, Rosebank, Johannesburg 2196, South Africa

Penguin Books Ltd, Registered Offices: 80 Strand, London WC2R ORL, England

www.penguin.com

First published by Penguin Ireland 2010
Published in Penguin Books 2011
1

Copyright © Simon Kelly, 2010
All rights reserved

The moral right of the author has been asserted

Set in Bembo Book MT Std
Typeset by Palimpsest Book Production Limited, Falkirk, Stirlingshire
Printed in Great Britain by Clays Ltd, St Ives plc

ISBN: 978-0-141-39961-4

www.greenpenguin.co.uk

This book is dedicated to Paddy Kelly,
my friend and father

Contents

Prologue

Early February 2009

I was sitting at the boardroom table in 128 Baggot Street, surveying the financial storm that was blowing all around me, when Claire Callanan phoned. Claire was the litigation partner in charge of our business affairs, and I had skipped her calls a few times because she never brought good news. Now it was getting worse.

'This time it's serious,' she told me. She asked me to come see her in her office at Beauchamps solicitors.

I drove to Beauchamps' offices on Sir John Rogerson's Quay. The building is a symbol of the property bubble, an edifice of glass and steel called Riverside 2 that stands proudly over the river Liffey. It was completed in 2006 and I was one of the developers. Sometimes it seemed that we were everybody's landlord.

I drive an old Black Land Rover Defender – 'the tractor', as my friends call it – and I squeezed into the basement car park cursing the pipes and ducts that skimmed the roof of the car. I jumped out and bounced up the glass stairs to Beauchamps' first-floor reception area, announcing my arrival with a smile to the receptionist. The staff knew me well and it felt as though I'd been there a million times. The wait in Reception was never long.

Claire came to collect me and we walked through to one of the meeting rooms overlooking the river. I could see the site of the new Anglo Irish Bank headquarters across the water, about midway between the International Financial

Services Centre and the port in the north docklands. Not for the first time, I thought: Why there?

In the chase to secure Anglo as a tenant, I had offered them a great site on the south docks across from the IFSC. It would have been sweet to be Anglo's landlord. We could easily have matched any offer that Liam Carroll made them. In the end, though, they had chosen his site, at the windy remote end of the north docks, as the winning location. That seemed strange to me. The joke around town was that they had chosen to move northside to be closer to Malahide, where David Drumm, their chief executive, lived. Either way, I had lost the competition and they were headed for Carroll's building.

The meeting rooms in Beauchamps are simple but comfortable, and I was offered fresh coffee and a few biscuits. Claire, as businesslike as ever in her suit, sat me down. We were joined by our barrister, James Doherty, who was looking sharp but a little nervous.

'We have a problem, Simon,' Claire said.

'I know,' I told her.

'Have you read what he wants?'

'He' was Hugh McGivern, my old nemesis. Almost a year previously, Hugh had taken me to the Commercial Court over a dispute relating to our joint involvement in the Mango fashion chain. He was a seasoned court campaigner, and I went down spectacularly in flames during the case, only narrowly avoiding a contempt action by the sitting judge, Peter Kelly. It was my first real outing in court and I had learned a few hard lessons about the theatre of it all.

Hugh's new action was against my father and business partner, Paddy Kelly, over unpaid rent on a Mango store in Belfast. The amount was small, only about £100,000, but the implications were huge. We would be up in front of Judge Kelly again. Things did not look good. I think Hugh believed that by threatening to bring down Paddy Kelly, he would force Anglo, our main lender, to come up with the missing rent in order to keep the show on the road.

Throughout 2008, Anglo had supported us with a restructuring and survival plan: they had provided the cash we needed to keep our business afloat while we tried to sell assets. The idea was that if our largest creditor backed us to the hilt, smaller creditors, like McGivern and other banks, would hold off from taking us to court. I had been pretty sure that this plan was doomed to fail from early on, but we stuck with it until it unravelled with the nationalization of Anglo in January 2009.

The plan had secured our liquidity, but now we had no liquidity. We couldn't repay Hugh McGivern or anyone else.

As part of his action, McGivern was seeking a court order forcing Paddy to lodge a statement of assets and liabilities. It was the latter issue that had Claire so animated.

'He'll put Paddy on the stand, Simon,' she said.

I think that Claire wanted us to fight, but our plan was different. If we couldn't borrow a bit more money from Anglo – and that looked likely – we were going to take this judgment and whatever else followed with dignity and honesty. We knew the system was completely bust and was going to collapse. There was too much debt and it could not be repaid. We were willing to go first, if we had to, and we knew we would not be last. We had led from the front on the way up in the boom and now it looked like Hugh McGivern was forcing us to lead from the front on the way down. Now that Anglo had abandoned us, we had no other choice.

Over the previous twelve months, I had researched and analysed all the options. I had spoken to insolvency experts. The only piece of legislation I have ever fully read is the 1988

Bankruptcy Act, and I had had a version of it saved on my laptop since early 2008. I had been telling everybody to read it.

I told Claire the plan. 'We're going to consent to the judgments, and admit to the court that we're broke and our liabilities exceed our assets. Paddy wants to be honest and open, and doesn't want to be accused of any kind of deceit. We're going to say that we're considering a scheme of arrangement under the 1988 Bankruptcy Act.' A scheme of arrangement is like an examinership for personal debts. Because our business was personal, and our debts secured with personal guarantees, we did not have the option of examinership, and a scheme was the next best thing. It would have given us full protection from all our creditors for a period of time while we arranged a vote on our survival.

We were willing to admit our financial failure in court, but we would have preferred to have more time and avoid the court spotlight. Over the next thirty minutes we drafted the replying affidavit to the McGivern action. In the back of my mind, I hoped that the honesty and directness of the affidavit might put Hugh off from pushing ahead for a judgment. Any intelligent person could see that the developers were in big trouble, and that this included Paddy and Simon Kelly.

At an earlier stage in the property crash, I had been up for fighting the banks. I had tried that with the Thomas Read examinership process and failed. I had put together a consortium to buy Thomas Read, a pub and restaurant group, from Hugh O'Regan in 2006. At the time, this business was heavily leveraged and we had been unable to refinance the debt. ACC Bank had refused to restructure the company debt to allow the business to survive, and we were forced into examinership – the first large company to go along this path since the beginning of the downturn. We tried to get the court to write our debts way down, but we failed and a receiver was appointed.

I had learned that energy and aggression stood for nothing when you were taking on the banks. This time, we would not fight a worthless fight. 'First in, first out,' was now our motto. While everybody else was fighting to avoid the crisis, we would be regrouping for the future.

The affidavit was finished overnight and emailed to me for approval. I read it a few times. The words were simple yet their implications were immense.

'My liabilities exceed my assets,' it said. 'We are examining our options under the 1988 Bankruptcy Act,' it added.

If Paddy Kelly could go, anybody could go. The banks could go and the whole system could go. We operated in a large number of partnerships with a wide range of people so I was aware of their finances in detail. Over the years of the boom, I had seen mountains of debt being given to a small group of developers. Once the music stopped and asset prices plunged, this debt was bound to cause serious problems. By the time we were in court with Hugh, the banks had already been guaranteed and Anglo had already been nationalized, so the process was well under way.

The act of signing the affidavit and sending it to Hugh McGivern was completed. Our next stop was to warn our banks of what we were going to do.

16 March 2009

Paddy and I lined up a meeting with Pat Whelan, the head of banking at Anglo, before our court hearing later that day. For property developers borrowing from Anglo, Pat was the single most important person in the bank. Drumm as CEO and Sean FitzPatrick as chairman got all the glamour, but the king for us was Pat. He was in charge of the money, and his approval would get almost any deal done.

The walk from our office in Baggot Street to Anglo's offices on St Stephen's Green took five minutes. I had done it thousands of times before, but this time it felt different. Anglo was now owned by the state and all flexibility had gone.

I had put on a dark suit for the meeting and the subsequent court hearing. Anglo people used to joke that when I wore a suit they knew it was serious.

We huddled around a small circular table in one of the many identical meeting rooms in the Anglo building, with a platter of sandwiches from O'Brien's, and told Pat about the court action and our strategy. I was due in the Commercial Court – a fast-track branch of the High Court for big-money business cases – at two p.m. We felt we had a small hope of a last-minute reprieve from our once-mighty bank. More realistically, we wanted to make sure that Pat and Anglo were OK with us talking about a scheme of arrangement. If we went into a scheme, we would need Anglo's support, and we did not want to presume that this would be available. We were sensitive to their needs, as they had been sensitive to ours in 2008.

Pat left us in no doubt that he could not lend any more money. We told him we were going to consent to the judgment.

'At the end of this, we can all plaster the walls with judgments,' he told us.

We were of the same view. The court process would result in mounds of paper, but nothing tangible. There would be lots of games left to play. A scheme of arrangement can be designed to leave you with certain assets; once we accepted our fate in court, the next phase of the plan would be to save what we could. We would move from trying to save everything to trying to save something.

We discussed the market and business in general, and the news seemed to be getting worse at Pat's end.

'There are clients I thought I would never see coming in saying they've lost all their money with CFDs,' Pat told us, referring to contracts for difference – a high-risk way of betting on shares that I had dabbled in myself. We all knew the developers were bust, but Pat was clearly referring to real clients with real money.

I left the meeting to rush to court. Now we were going across the line into formal insolvency and there would be fireworks.

'Don't be late or Justice Kelly will kill you,' Claire screamed at me down the phone.

I jumped into a taxi on the Green. Paddy would follow later. 'Four Courts,' I said.

It was a sunny day, and Dublin was decorated for the St Patrick's festival. I arrived at the courts a few minutes late. It was only a short walk from the security gate to Court Fourteen.

I always feel excitement in the air prior to a court appearance. Both sides can see each other huddled in the hall outside the courtroom discussing strategy. Our case had been delayed until about three p.m., and there was some last-minute behind-the-scenes chat between the legal teams.

We wanted to get in and out of court as quickly as possible, and presenting a statement of affairs – which was what Hugh was looking for – would be the start of a court circus that would run and run. The court process is public and our statement of affairs would feed the newspapers for weeks. It would also reveal the problems of our various business partners.

A kind of compromise was reached. Hugh would pull back from seeking the statement of affairs, but would push ahead in pursuit of a judgment.

We slipped into the courtroom. I headed for the back row, sitting behind Hugh McGivern and his solicitor.

Claire sat in beside me. 'Is your phone off? Kelly will kill you if it rings,' she said.

'Yes,' I replied. 'I have been here before, you know.'

I found myself hoping that Hugh's phone would ring. In fact I was tempted to nip out and give him a call.

Our case was called just as Paddy slipped in. Apart from our lawyers, and the McGivern team, the courtroom was virtually empty: it was a slow week because of St Patrick's Day. Ours was the last case of the session. The sun was shining through the large windows and the room had a surreal air. My mind flashed back to the previous McGivern case, which had taken place in this very room. They were not fond memories.

James Doherty, our barrister, stood up and told Justice Kelly that the legal teams had reached an agreement. We had consented to the judgments as requested and the motion for a statement of affairs to be lodged to the court had been stayed for two weeks while further discussions took place.

It was a simple and solemn affair. Justice Kelly made what was for him a short speech, but he stirred it up a little by worrying out loud about a 'rush to judgment by Paddy Kelly's other creditors'.

There were no journalists in the courtroom and we were not approached by anybody after the hearing. I shook hands with Claire and our legal team. Then Paddy and I drove back to the office together. Dublin was quiet. The court had been so empty and the hearing so fast that I wondered if anybody would pick up on the news. We drove away not knowing what was to follow in the days ahead.

Paddy was flying to Belgium with my mum the next morning to visit the hotel business we had there. We were both pretty tired from the preparations for the court case so we did not talk much in the car.

I jumped out of Paddy's car and into mine and started my drive to Wicklow. I was looking forward to a nice St Patrick's Day with my wife and our four children.

Little did I know that things would start moving really fast.

1. The Beginning

From a young age, it was my destiny to become a property developer.

Paddy, my father, was one of eight sons born to Christopher and Mary Kelly, and almost all of them worked in property in some manner. C. Kelly and Sons had been a contracting business, and this had turned into a development business when Paddy and his brothers moved to Dublin in the 1960s. Ireland was coming out of its economic shell and people like my father and his brothers felt as though they were literally building the country from the ground up.

Even then, boom-and-bust was an established way of life. Around the time I was born, in 1971, Paddy was dealing with his first business solvency crisis: C. Kelly and Sons was just successfully emerging from a scheme of arrangement.

In September 1985, when I was a fourteen-year-old computer nut, I accompanied my father to a meeting with the mighty ICI Computer Company at their impressive offices in Reading. At that time ICI were purveyors of 'big iron' computers to corporate Britain. I was introduced as the computer guy, and the ICI men laughed. They presumed Paddy was joking, but it was no joke.

The ICI guys were impressive in their slick double-breasted suits: in the mid-1980s, dressing like a stockbroker was the name of the game, even for computer salesmen. We were shown the latest technology and software systems. Paddy and his construction manager walked ICI through the scale of their UK property-development operation. Reading Estates

Ltd had been born in the mid-1980s as a joint venture between my father and Brian Kelly (no relation), a property developer and businessman from Dublin. The company grew fast and boomed along with the rest of the UK in the 1980s. It had five sites under construction in the Reading area for apartments, offices and factories, and ambitions to grow fast.

The business was partly run from Ireland. Paddy would fly to Heathrow every Monday morning, paying Aer Lingus about £200 for the privilege of leaving the island. There were plenty of other Irish developers at the time whose main work was across the water, and that Monday-morning flight had become a bit like a club. Ireland was dead to all of them as a business location, and the UK was heading for the moon. Margaret Thatcher's government was promoting home ownership. Everybody who owned their home would vote Conservative, she reckoned. Reading Estates wanted to build as many of these homes as possible.

The meeting went on for about an hour and I could see the computer salesmen salivating at the prospect of a big sale. They planned to establish a permanent dedicated telephone line under the Irish Sea to connect to Paddy in Dublin. Towards the end of the meeting we got down to the question of money. The turnover of Reading Estates at the time was about £3 million a year and rising fast. The salesmen latched on to this and went in for the kill. A company of our stature, they said, would need to have an IT budget of 1 per cent of turnover: £30,000. I was fourteen years old and £30,000 seemed like all the money in the world to me. I couldn't believe that computers could cost £30,000, and I certainly couldn't believe that we were going to spend that amount on them.

The meeting ended with the usual promises of more meetings and returned phone calls. We walked out on to the high street and Paddy asked me what I thought.

'We need to buy an Amstrad,' I said.

There was no more discussion: we walked up the street to the nearest Dixons store. Dixons was the top gadget retailer in the 1980s and it was my Mecca. It stocked all the newest and best electronic things and I could spend hours there looking at them. This visit was brief, as we knew what we wanted: earlier that year, Amstrad had launched their PCW personal computer. We walked straight up to the counter and purchased one, with a copy of Supercalc II, its spreadsheet software. The total bill was £395.

That was the moment when my world met the developers' world. Paddy always wanted the numbers, the what-ifs and the why-nots. I just wanted to play with computers. I could do the numbers that would answer the what-ifs.

We got into the car and drove straight to the site office: a bland ground-floor apartment in a development the company had just built on the outskirts of Reading. This was where the new technology was revealed to all. I can remember the gasps of amazement when people saw the power of spreadsheets for the first time. The property men were used to calculating the numbers on the back of an envelope. With the spreadsheet models built and running, we started to change everything in the business and plan new ways to make money.

I spent a lot of time in Reading that summer, modelling the various developments, with Paddy looking over my shoulder making adjustments to the numbers. 'Change the yield, and push the rent,' he might say. Or: 'We need to reduce the WIP figure.'

WIP (work in progress), yield, PSF (per square foot), build cost, leverage, profit, cash flow, margin on cost – these all became common terms and formulas for me in my early teens. Today this kind of number-crunching power is everywhere, but in 1985, in Reading on a wet Saturday, it was mind-blowing. I now had a place in the business. I was the 'numbers guy'. You came to me if you wanted your numbers done.

Analysis gave us options, and options gave us plans, and plans were what the banks wanted. They had computers too, but the managers did not know how to use them and they were not spreadsheet jockeys. We could out-crunch them, and they gave the money willingly. Reading Estates was becoming a large business in the UK boom of the 1980s. Its profits were high, and so were its debts. At its peak the business had a value of £20 million and it was poised to float on the stock market. This did not come to pass, as the crash of the late 1980s destroyed the property developers and their business. Land values crashed because no bank debt was available. The UK banks pulled the trigger on all developers and swamped the market with land for sale, for which there were no buyers. I remember a site in Chiswick that had cost £2 million being sold for £400,000. Twenty pence in the pound was where values settled. As with the current crash in Ireland, the banks had received personal guarantees from developers on their loans. Paddy had signed his fair share of these and, when the crash came, they came home to roost.

If that was not bad enough, Lloyds of London had collapsed in a mire of debt and was seeking £4 million from my parents. Lloyds was an old London institution where the world's re-insurance was written. The company had no capital of its own, and it relied on the personal guarantees of its members in the event that cash was needed. At no time in the past had those guarantees ever been called upon, but that had changed now. My parents were both members, and the bill had now arrived.

That was when I had my lesson from Paddy in dealing with debt. The first rule was that we would not hide from it. The second was that we would not let it get in the way of us

making money again. We happily produced the figures for
all the UK banks showing that we were insolvent due to the
Lloyds losses. In the bankers' mind, a connection to Lloyds
meant certain death, from a financial point of view, and they
wanted to get away from us as fast as they could.

We settled the bank debts for less than 10p in the pound on
monthly schedules, paying about £3,000 per month in total.
We also settled the Lloyds debt of £4 million for about
£330,000. Those lessons were fundamental to my upbringing.
Life was comfortable as a developer, but it was never easy.
You made money and you lost money. Nobody was ever
your enemy, and you would sit down with everybody and
anybody to help the deal along. The past was the past, and
the future was all that really counted. You had to have a
razor-sharp ability to cut through bullshit, and this set you
apart from the rest of the market.

The other lesson I took from this episode was about the
flexibility of debt. Bond-market debt is a flexible asset, with
its price rising and falling based on the likelihood of repay-
ment and the health of the underlying business. Our debt
came from banks, not bondholders, but I learned to view it
in a similar manner. The bank statement might say £1 million
but this did not mean that you could not settle for less. After
the 1980s crash in the UK, Paddy owed development-land
debt to a number of UK banks in relation to collapsed property projects. In all cases, those banks were only too happy
to accept reduced settlement terms. We funded the settle-
ments over two or three years with the early profits that were
starting to emerge from the Irish property business.

Of course, it wasn't always possible to count on the flexibility of debt. It was around this time that AIB pursued
Paddy, because they had provided him with a £250,000 bank
guarantee to support his Lloyds membership. This guarantee

had been triggered, and AIB were now calling to get paid. The family home, at Shrewsbury Road in Dublin, was sacrificed to settle that one.

I also learned that one good deal could rebuild the whole business, despite the problems with failed projects. What counted was to keep going and keep looking forward. Banks have short memories – their need for profit has that effect – and they will always deal with you again.

After we bought that first Amstrad, I spent the next five years working with Paddy in the evenings at home. My friends would work in bars for £1.20 per hour in wages, with maybe a tip; I was working from home, charging £7.50 per hour, crunching the numbers. That was a fortune for me, though I never really did it for the money then, and I certainly never charged for all the hours I worked. I did it for the buzz and excitement I got from working on large business deals with my dad, and on the computers and spreadsheets, which I loved.

I used to work from my bedroom because that was where the computers were. I had a long built-in kitchen counter full of papers, and a big computer and a wide-format printer that could churn out spreadsheets. Somewhere on the floor there was some undone homework: business came first and school a distant second. Homework could wait till the morning because I did the number-crunching with Paddy in the evening. From the very start it was a partnership. Everything was a partnership for Paddy. Nobody was the boss and nobody the employee. Paddy and I spoke a common language called 'property', and we both knew what we were talking about.

I finished school in 1990 and did not want to go to college – I had probably seen too much of the business world to go into the academic one. I went to London and took a number of jobs, from selling newspapers in Selfridges to computer number-crunching for the old men of Royal Insurance International in the City. I still did the numbers for Paddy in my spare time. Uncles would visit me in London and we would get out the laptop to have a look at a project. Paddy would fly me home so we could get a few days together updating the models on some sites. The property world, where we discussed things in hundreds of thousands and millions, was a lot more attractive than the nine-to-five world, where I thought in tens and hundreds.

I returned home in 1994. The back of the garage in Shrewsbury Road had been turned into a small office for the business. (We had sacrificed our original house on Shrewsbury Road to AIB, then built a new one in the garden and this was where the office was. We called it Lloyds Lodge.) I was the only employee (or partner, as Paddy would say) at the time and I started on a salary of £1,000 per month. I was ready to work full-time in property and Dublin was ready for the dawn of the developers.

It was around this time that I had my first breakfast with Anglo.

We were building 25,000 square feet of offices in three blocks behind the shops on the main street in Dundrum. We had formed a company called Heritage Holdings Ltd to carry out the project. The site had been bought from Hugh McGivern and the McGrane brothers, for a small amount of money, and the part swap of two one-bed apartments on Francis Street. That was how all the early deals were done. Nobody had the money to walk in and do a simple deal: instead we relied on barter and creativity.

Part of the land-purchase deal was that the McGrane brothers would acquire Block 3 for a fixed and discounted price.

We then pre-sold Block 1 to Dun Laoghaire–Rathdown
County Council. That left Block 2 in the middle to be built
'on spec' – without any tenants or purchasers lined up. It
takes time to get something built, sometimes up to two years,
and spec building plays on the impatience of the Irish. When
we want something, we want it now – not in two years' time.
By going ahead with construction in the absence of a
purchaser or tenants, the developer takes a big risk – but he
also improves his chances of getting a deal done.

In Dundrum our timing was not great, but we were grinding out deals with tenants and purchasers one by one, hence
my need for a chat with Anglo. Anglo were funding the deal,
but we did not have a wrapped-up facility in place. The bank
facilities for these early deals were not as formal as they
became in later years, and every drawdown involved a negotiation. When we wanted to discuss an issue with Anglo and
get some money released, we went to breakfast.

That first breakfast, for me, was at the café in Dundrum
where we carried out our meetings for the project. It was
small but it served big helpings. Full Irish was the standard
order, with rounds of buttered toast and hot tea. The tables
were too close together and smoke filled the room.

Pat Whelan, our senior lender in Anglo, was sending out
David Drumm, his new young gun, to discuss the loan and
look at the site with us. Paddy had met him before, but this
was my first time. 'Look after David and work well together,'
Pat had told us, 'because the bank has faith in him and he's
going places.'

I think Anglo were a little unsure as to what Paddy was up
to in Dundrum even though they were financing the project.
David Drumm was being sent to get to know the deal. Anglo
was the only bank in Dublin willing to finance speculative
development for us, so I knew we had to keep them happy.

They were the only show in town. It would be years before I even went to another bank about a deal. With Anglo on board, there was no need to talk to the others.

I had done the numbers and the deal was fine. The pre-sale of Blocks 1 and 3 took most of the risk out of the project, and the main task from there was to sell the remaining units in Block 2. The numbers were good and David was happy. That did not mean that the money would be easy. It was early days and the money was never easy. Anglo was built on lending as little money as possible, and always getting it back, plus interest and fees. Property development in the mid-1990s was all about getting the deal done, the building up and sold, and the money back in the bank. We had very limited capital so we had to recycle it as fast as we could. Anglo, similarly, had very little cash and needed to keep the repayments coming in as fast as possible.

At breakfast, Paddy told David that I would be handling and reporting on the numbers henceforth. David was fine with this. If Paddy trusted me, David trusted me. Paddy had always told me that the trick to being a good developer was to stay away from the site, and close to the bank. The most important part of a development is finance, not the buildings: they should look after themselves once you have a good architect and design team.

At that first meeting I was very impressed by David. I had not met a lot of bankers yet, but I knew immediately that he was different. I presumed that bankers would be stuffy and dull, but he was the exact opposite. He was funny and very clever. He had confidence in himself, the bank and its business, which was immediately obvious. I soon learned that this confidence filled the whole bank. Anglo was the underdog taking on the big boys, and they loved this role. We had a similar attitude, and it began to feel like a joint mission.

During the meeting we went through the numbers in detail and I was left in no doubt that David, too, was a numbers guy. He had a speed of mind and business logic that I would meet again and again from the Anglo bankers. And he knew how to laugh – another characteristic of Anglo bankers. They were easy to like.

Initially we had hoped that a single tenant or purchaser would turn up for Block 2, but this did not happen. The big-fish tenants did not arrive on the scene till later in the boom. As a result, Block 2 was broken up into small individual units and we wrapped up the Dundrum project with a series of deals over a few months.

That deal and others in those days produced very little profit. The bank was paid and the creditors were paid, but there was not much for us. Construction costs were beginning to move upwards and that always meant profit erosion in a project. Some projects would pre-sell the entire stock of apartments prior to starting construction, but in the time between sales and starting on site, construction inflation would have risen by 15–20 per cent and the profit would have vanished. The fear of inflation began to put developers off pre-selling too much product, and this gave rise to higher-risk speculative development.

Dundrum had a silver lining because we had retained a 400-metre strip of the old Harcourt Street rail line; a few years later we sold this to the state for over €1 million for the construction of the Luas line.

I remember speaking to my father on the phone from London in the early 1990s. He would tell me of this wondrous place called Tallaght. It sounded like heaven – until I got there.

Tallaght was a small village south-west of Dublin that was

turning into a big town. The Square Shopping Centre had landed there as if from space and seemed to have set off a chain reaction of development. Paddy had agreed to buy about seven acres in Tallaght from Dublin County Council. We paid a small deposit on the land and passed over the balance of the money as the development – the Tallaght Retail Centre – progressed.

The project was slow going. We were building the scheme in seven phases, trying to complete each one before we started the next. The site was a mix of offices, small shops and big-box retail units. Big-box retailing was unheard of in Ireland when we started Tallaght, and the UK retailers had not yet arrived on the scene. That left us dealing with a limited number of potential tenants who might be willing to take a risk and open a store in Tallaght.

Tallaght was important in the overall story of the boom because it was where a lot of the early developers cut their teeth. The rise of Anglo Irish Bank, and of professional investors like Derek Quinlan, was closely connected with the construction blitz there. There was plenty of land and there were plenty of people to work. What was needed were the buildings, the infrastructure and the multinational companies.

Urban-renewal tax breaks drove everything in Tallaght and occupied most of our discussions. The incentives had been put in place in 1987 to encourage the development of run-down parts of Dublin and Ireland. They worked like this. For tenants there was double rent relief, which could be offset against all forms of income. That meant that a tenant who paid £100 in rent could charge £200 in their accounts. With a prevailing tax rate of about 50 per cent, the rent of £100 was offset by the tax saving of £100. In effect, the shop or office was free if you had profits to shelter. In addition to this incentive, there were no council rates in Tallaght for the initial ten years. That was great for tenants with profitable businesses elsewhere in Dublin. It also allowed us to push up the rent.

There were not a lot of investors in the Irish property market at the time, and this meant that there were not a lot of buyers for the shops and offices we were developing. Again, tax breaks created the market. A buyer of a building in Tallaght would receive a tax break based upon the cost of the shop or office. Four-fifths of the cost could be offset against other forms of income, including your salary.

A group of investors would get together to buy a shop or office for, say, £100,000. The rent on that kind of development would have been between £8,000 and £10,000. The investor would receive a tax break of £80,000 against their tax bill, which translated to a tax saving of about £40,000. The tax saving would form the deposit on the shop, and a bank would lend the balance of £60,000. The result of this was that you got the shop for free, and the tenant would pay off the bank loan. As values soared, a lot of people made a lot of money in Tallaght, but not developers like us. We missed out on most of the big profits because we were selling all of the units to pay back the bank debt. With inflation beginning to accelerate, the real money was made by buying and holding on to property, rather than building and selling. We did not have this option because Anglo always needed the money back and could not provide long-term finance.

Many of the large deals were made by groups of investors led by Derek Quinlan. We would do a deal with Derek to sell a building, and at the closing we would finally get to see who the investors were. Tallaght was a great place to shelter your income from tax, and I doubt those investors spent much time there studying their investments. Looking at the lower tax bill was probably much more fun.

The partners in the Tallaght Retail Centre deal were Jarlath Sweeney, John Walsh, John McCabe and ourselves. Each of us had our role: John Walsh was the tenant-hunter, John McCabe was the builder, Paddy handled the financing, while Jarlath and I looked after the numbers and other details.

We were not out to win any awards in terms of the architecture.

We had constructed a large building, of which Smyths Toys took the ground floor for a shop. We had built the upper floors to sell on spec and we were not sure what to do with them.

The squeeze came from Anglo every March to get deals closed for April: buildings had to be sold by 5 April to be allowed in that year's tax returns. Most years I was up till midnight on 5 April getting deals over the line. That day happens to be my wife's birthday, and every year I would promise to get home so we could go to dinner, but that never happened. I was one of the happiest people in Ireland when the tax-year end was moved to 31 December.

With the Anglo squeeze on, we used to sell buildings vacant with a rent guarantee in place. In effect, we would put down three or four years' rent as a guarantee to the buyer; we'd then hope that we could rent it for real. We did this with the upper floors of the Smyths Toys building, which we sold to a syndicate managed by Alanis, an investment vehicle of the McCormack family. The McCormacks were a professional family pulled into the property world by the lure of big profits. John McCormack, the father, had been the managing director of Property Loan and Investment Company, a subsidiary of the Bank of Ireland Group. In the early days, he would arrange for investors to buy into property deals, taking a share of the up-side. John's sons, Brian, Niall and Alan, subsequently entered the business and drove it into the property-development sector. By the end of the boom, they were among Ireland's largest developers.

Anglo was happy that we'd done the deal with Alanis, because another tranche of our debt was paid off. The rent had been struck at a low level to make the deal fly; now we had to get busy and let the building at a higher level if we were going to make any profit. A pile of double-height office space above a toy shop in Tallaght is not exactly prime property.

John Walsh was a legendary tenant-hunter. He would travel around Tallaght on a tour bus with the IDA and executives visiting from America. They were looking for office locations in Ireland and we always made sure they got to Tallaght early in the tour. Tax rates for companies were low in Ireland, as were wages, and the foreign direct investment boom was starting.

In 1996 John came upon UPS, who were seeking a European call centre, and there was no way he was going to let them off the hook. Tallaght had a good telecoms infrastructure, which was vital to call-centre operators and the key to their choice of location. We did a deal to lease them the first floor above Smyths at twice the rent we were paying to the McCormack syndicate. We had about six weeks to get the building ready for UPS to move in, which meant we had to start immediately.

Nowadays regulations, fire certificates and planning permission would get in the way of this kind of quick build, but that was the dynamic Ireland of the 1990s. Paddy went to see Pat Rabbitte, the local Labour TD and junior government minister, about the project. We were bringing hundreds of jobs to Tallaght, so he was over the moon. Fire ahead, he told us, and I'll sort out the planning and other issues. There were no brown-paper bags, but people were happy to go the extra

mile for the greater good of the area and jobs. We were given
the green light to proceed in advance of the planning permission so that the jobs were secured. Jobs were what the
politicians wanted in their area and new buildings would lead
to them.

We pushed ahead with the fit-out work. With the works
nearing completion and UPS getting ready to move in, we
hit a roadblock. Brian McCormack, we were told, was not
happy to have UPS as a sub-tenant. He threatened to get a
court injunction to prevent the tenant entering the building
and taking up occupation. We were well into our fit-out, and
UPS were due to take occupation any day now. The new
staff had been hired. We did not need this, and I was shocked
by Brian's threatened action. Tallaght was a real place with
real people, and these jobs were important – as was our
profit.

Paddy woke me early by tapping on the window of my
apartment when he heard this news. We convened in the
offices of our solicitors, BCM Hanby Wallace, and prepared
to go into battle. It was going to be my first experience in
court and I was really excited. I had never met Brian McCormack, but I had formed a picture of a monster. We would
later become great partners. As a developer, you can make a
friend of an enemy – and an enemy of a friend.

We presumed that Brian was going to present himself at
the Four Courts with his barrister and seek the injunction.
We knew that if it was to happen it would be on that day
because UPS were turning the building on the following
day.

Our strategy was to head to the courts with our solicitors
and barrister and make our presence felt. If the McCormacks
attacked we were going to defend and fight back. We walked
down to the courts and spread out to see if we could find

Brian and his legal team. We also wanted word to filter back
that we were down in the courts and ready for a fight.

We could not find Brian or his legal team. Paddy made a
phone call to John McCormack, Brian's father and the cool
head in their business. In his characteristic style, Paddy asked
John if he needed help coming down from the high ledge.
He suspected that Brian's bark was worse than his bite. John
agreed to a meeting later that day.

Paddy travelled out to the Alanis offices in the Stillorgan
Shopping Centre, which they managed for the Bank of
Ireland pension fund. A deal was swiftly reached whereby
they would buy the UPS deal from us at market rates. It was
a fair solution to a simple problem. UPS were able to take
up their tenancy, and we even managed to make a small profit.

The victory turned sour when we went for a drink to
celebrate the deal at Kiely's pub in Donnybrook. John Walsh
and Jarlath Sweeney were celebrating our success and retelling
the story of how Paddy had faced down the McCormacks.
After a few drinks, Jarlath excused himself to the bathroom.
When he didn't come back, John went to look for him and
found him on the floor. Jarlath was dispatched to St Vincent's
in an ambulance. I thought there was a direct link between
his collapse and the stress of the UPS rental dispute. This
incident caused Jarlath to take a back seat in the partnership
and he ultimately retired from it to settle into a more sedate
development and hotel business in Bray with his wife,
Lorraine. From today's viewpoint, it was a very wise move
as he missed both the boom and the bust.

Dundrum and Tallaght were my training grounds in the
property-development business in Ireland. We handled large
sums of money and we did a lot of deals to lease and sell
buildings. Nothing was easily earned and some things had to

be fought over. The sum total in profits from all this development and activity was close to zero, but we had a team together and we had a base to work off. We had proven to Anglo Irish Bank that we could grind out the results to get them their money back, plus fees and interest.

I had been in the property business for over ten years at this stage and I was only twenty-five years old. I had seen the grind of trying to get things started in a bad economy in Dundrum and Tallaght, and I had also seen what happens when the market goes wrong, as it did in the UK in the late 1980s. I felt that I was now armed and trained in most of the arts of development. I had seen grown men cry over money problems, but never us. We were stronger than that.

2. Working with Anglo

I could never get my timing quite right. I was due to meet
Kieran Duggan from Anglo at seven a.m. for breakfast at the
No. 27 restaurant in Dublin's Shelbourne Hotel. I set my
alarm for six, giving me plenty of time to shower, shave,
dress and make the short walk from Lad Lane. The alarm
went off and I hit the snooze button before it woke Joanna.
(This was never actually a problem – she could sleep through
anything.) I love the feeling of half-sleep, knowing you have
to get up but wallowing in doziness.

Some days I dress like a tramp, and others like an investment banker. That day felt like an investment-banker day, so
after my shower I put on a suit. As I headed for the door I
heard a call from upstairs.

'Can you make tea before you go?' Joanna hollered down.

'Okay,' I called back, knowing it was going to make me
late. Always late . . .

I boiled the kettle and it took an age, but at last I arrived
upstairs with tea.

'Who are you meeting?' Joanna asked, without opening
her eyes.

'Kieran from Anglo.'

'You're always meeting Anglo,' she mumbled.

I kissed her goodbye, then headed downstairs and out
into the street. As usual, it was wet and the lane looked
dirty. Lad Lane in the morning always seems to show
evidence of illicit behaviour from the night before. Invariably somebody seems to have forgotten to take their clothes

home. Jackets and ties can be found in the funniest places and you have to watch your step. I enjoyed the walk, and that morning Dublin was quiet and rainswept. At the door, I tossed up my options.

Lad Lane or Fitzwilliam Square? The walk through the square added a few minutes and I was already late, but Lad Lane was not as nice. The square it was and I turned right out the door. I texted Kieran – *There in 5 mins. Sorry. Simon* – so he wouldn't worry, though I knew it would take me ten. Always late . . .

I turned out of Cumberland Road on to Fitzwilliam Square and started down Fitzwilliam Street. What a beautiful view you got from Fitzwilliam Square down to Holles Street: whenever I walked that route, I felt privileged to live and work in the town – Dublin, the centre of the world.

The streets were empty and by ten past seven I knew I was going to be my usual fifteen minutes late. The Simon Kelly factor, as they used to say in the office.

Joanna used to tell me I was way too busy. Too many deals and too many balls in the air. 'You'll drop them in the end,' she'd say.

'Don't be silly,' I'd tell her. 'It'll be better once I get this one sorted.' Looking back now, I realize you can make yourself believe anything. Once 'this one' was sorted, there was always another.

Through the square and past the McCormacks' office – I glanced to see if they were in. It was generally too early for them but some days they were there at this hour, churning away with the lights on. I had never seen them at breakfast in the Shelbourne, so they must have had a different routine.

Turning on to Baggot Street, I put on my game face and got into the zone. Baggot Street was empty. Nobody else was up at that hour, trying to borrow more money from Anglo, it seemed. One or two shops were getting ready to open and the pavement was strewn with early-morning deliveries.

In the final stretch I ran over the various projects in my mind. Would Kieran have any difficult questions? I made a mental rundown of the issues. I didn't need notes – it was all in my head. Every detail of every project. Value, rent, square footage, budget, everything. There was always the risk that he would have an agenda that might not suit my immediate need for more money.

The Shelbourne is an institution to many people for lots of different reasons, but for me it was where you borrowed the money from Anglo. No weddings or romance for me there, just money.

At that time Kieran was our main man in Anglo. Not everybody was lucky enough to get him. He was reserved for the loyal clients. The rest were left to play in the minor leagues with the wannabe Kierans. Asking for money was never easy, but Kieran made it feel easy. He never let me squirm on the question. Sometimes, when he felt my need, he even offered. He had a way of knowing when we needed his help, and I think he liked that power. A request for a breakfast meeting at the Shelbourne was a tacit way of getting Kieran ready for a funding request.

I had been at the game for just a few years, and I had not developed Paddy's straight-up approach to asking for loot. I still felt guilty about it.

I entered the hotel through the old revolving doors, gave the concierge a glance of acknowledgement and turned left into the restaurant. The fire in the lobby warmed the air and I immediately felt myself thawing.

Once I crossed the threshold, the warm glow and comfort of the No. 27 pulled me in. I relaxed and strode across the room to Kieran's table. Once, I saw Kieran there with another client and felt a sense of betrayal: that was our place, and it was not to be spoilt with other clients. We were special and we had the special relationship: loyal client with loyal bankers doing sensible business. As Kieran would say to me, 'We'll never discuss anything as vulgar as money.'

I liked this idea. We were above the money. We were creating, developing, building, and our goal was never the money. If not the money, who knows what? I didn't – but certainly never the money. We were after a higher purpose, or so we thought.

'Community and harmony,' Paddy would say.

On my way to the table I skirted around the buffet set up in the centre of the room, stacked high with muffins and pastries. The hot breakfast was stored in shining silver chafing dishes. Fresh fruit was spread out beside the cold meats and cheeses. Comfort and opulence were the order of the day. On my first visit there with Paddy, I tried the buffet, but I soon learned this was a schoolboy error. When we were there on bank business we ordered off the menu.

'Two poached eggs with bacon,' Kieran told the waitress. His order never changed. I learned to follow the master and ordered the same, with some juice and coffee. Shining silver pots of coffee, as much as you could drink, and fresh cups with every pot. We would get brown and white toast cut into triangles and served in silver toast racks, with little pots of jam and other toppings.

We opened with the usual small-talk.

'What's Treasury up to?'

'What's that site worth?'

'Did you hear how many units they sold at the launch?'

'What are the shares at?'

This was the kind of thing that all players in the market would discuss. There were no failures. There were only levels of success. To be in the Shelbourne, we had to be near the top.

The poached eggs were served on small circles of toast, and cooked to order. Medium was my preference and there would be a run of dark yellow yolk when I broke the thin outer layer. The bacon was always hot and crisp. The table was spacious and we spread out, eating and talking, figures at the ready. Always at the ready.

The talk of the deal didn't start until the food was finished and the second or third pot of coffee was on the table. We both knew we were there to discuss the money but enjoyed the meal first. It's always easier with the warm glow of good food energizing your body and filling your soul. I have no idea what it cost because I never paid. At the end, the Anglo credit card was handed over and it was as if the bill didn't exist.

The grind in Dundrum and Tallaght had positioned us to move to the big-time and try to make some serious money. In 1996 we joined up with the Flynns and the Linders to purchase land from the Jones Group plc at Clonskeagh in south County Dublin. The land was being sold by private treaty, which meant that it was being offered around the market. The Flynns were fellow developers and long-time partners of Paddy, and Joe Linders was another Dublin-based developer with a taste for office deals. We needed to put together this large group in order to get the deal financed. Also, Joe had been bidding separately for the land; involving him in our consortium was a way of eliminating a competitor. This land was to become Belfield Office Park and it was the deal that moved us to the big-time.

The Clonskeagh purchase was possible because of our small equity in Dundrum and Tallaght. Equity is the difference between the value of a building and the debt on it. Because the debt in any property deal is at a fixed level and the value of that property can rise with the market, our equity was continually growing – even in our sleep. That equity was not cash, but it gave us the wherewithal to borrow money with which we could expand the business. The more equity you had, the more money the banks would lend you. That was how a small number of developers grew to dominate the debt list in Anglo and the other banks. By starting early in the boom cycle and growing fast, the nature of the maths ensured that you ended up with the most assets and therefore the most debts – a perverted kind of early-mover advantage.

The general property-market view was that the site could accommodate 120,000 square feet of offices, but Paddy thought we could do three times this. Once we had purchased the site, we immediately set to work lodging our first planning application. We built on spec and in advance of planning permission to satisfy the tenants' needs and get the business done. Over a series of three further planning applications we gradually increased the size of the buildings, led by the tenants' needs. The final tenant list was impressive: we had secured Eircom, Compaq, Smartforce and the Office of Public Works, and sold a building to Ericsson. We took Belfield from a £3.25-million site and transformed it into a development of 369,000 square feet with a rent roll of close to £5 million and a value at the peak of over £100 million.

The development included an underground car park with space for at least a thousand cars. Basements in the suburbs were a new thing, and building one for cars was like buying more land: with the cars out of the way, the buildings could spread out and rise up. The anchor tenant for the scheme was Compaq, which was moving to Ireland to set up a base of operations. We were competing for them against the East

Point Office Park. To be able to chase a tenant you had to be on site building their proposed office in advance of the lease. This was the nature of the business: we had to take the risk, backed by Anglo, to build on spec in hope of securing the big tenant. The economy was moving very fast, with new tenants arriving into the country all the time, so this was a calculated risk. Anglo backed us in every way with this transaction, and together we generated a huge property asset with a lot of equity and profit. We also built up our credibility and mystique within the bank.

The lease we agreed with Compaq for Belfield Office Park was the largest letting ever done in Ireland to that point. Our target profit was £12 million; the actual profit was at least twice that. We massively over-achieved and this gave us a very powerful position in the market and with the bank. We were the clients that the bank wanted to nurture. We were loyal, too: we always acknowledged them as a partner in our business and we always told other prospective clients that they were the only bank worth dealing with.

AIB tried to finance the Belfield Office Park project and we allowed them to believe they had a chance at the deal. That was never the case, but we were happy to play with them a little. The memory of their legal action against Paddy because of Lloyds was still fresh in our minds. We let them get excited about the loan, and we took them all the way through the credit process and into legal preparation. In the end when Paddy told them he was sticking with Anglo, he gave them a simple reason: 'I can't trust you to keep your heads when we have a problem.'

There were always problems with development projects and we did not trust any bank apart from Anglo to be able to deal with these twists and turns. AIB had a terrible reputation for panicking, gained in the early 1990s during the currency crisis, and Bank of Ireland were too sleepy to do anything. John Flynn used to say that Anglo was the first bank to allow us to walk in the front door; Bank of Ireland and AIB sent developers to various sub-divisions and specialty sections. Developers were never invited into the old establishment banks, and Anglo built its whole business on dealing with them.

Pitching deals to the bank was simple. I knew what Anglo liked and it was the same thing that I liked: deals in familiar areas of southside Dublin. Nothing too exotic or edgy. There was no need to go too far from home to make money.

The deals came in a few different flavours and we tasted them all. At the plain-vanilla end there would be a plot of land that was in the papers and coming up for sale by tender. Most land was sold in this way during the boom because there were usually plenty of potential buyers around and the tender process was the best way to get them excited and focused on a fixed deadline. In order to tender for land, you needed to produce a bank draft on the tender date with the signed contract. This was where Anglo came into its own. The draft was generally for 10 per cent of the purchase price (or sometimes a fixed amount), and it was always a large sum of money. If the bid failed, the draft would be returned, but if you succeeded it would be lodged to the vendor's solicitor's account. Anglo was the easiest place to source a draft for your bid, and you knew that they would be able to follow up and finance the deal if you were successful. That was part of their unique service. The other banks were never as free with that kind of money.

There was an unwritten rule that said: 'If Anglo give you the deposit cheque, they get the debt for the deal.'

There was a lot of competition from banks to lend money to the big developers on the big deals, and I think Anglo's biggest fear was that they would lose clients and deals to the other banks who charged less. Anglo had always charged more for their money, but they won and kept clients by lending this money more easily than their competitors. As developers, we talked about the 'Anglo premium' all the time, and some chose to go elsewhere for lower interest rates and fees, but not many and certainly not us. We valued Anglo's flexibility and didn't mind paying for it. The Anglo premium was easily outweighed by the benefit of being able to do more deals.

When looking at a tender, we took account of a few basic kinds of information. Most players in the market had a pretty good idea of what the planners would allow on a site. The plot ratio is the ratio of building space to land area. An acre of land has about 43,500 square feet in it. Central Dublin could take a plot ratio of three, which meant that you could build about 120,000 square feet per acre, equating to about 120 apartments, if that was the use. The plot ratio would reduce to 0.5 as you moved out to the suburbs. These were not rigid rules, but they were guidelines that most local authorities adhered to. The zoning laws gave pretty clear guidance for permitted uses on sites. Land was generally for office, residential or hotel use, and often a mixed-use scheme would tick all the boxes. We loved a mixed-use scheme, and the planners usually did too.

The key differentiator in bidding for land was the type and cost of finance, and your view on future property values. It was a game of nerves. When the market heated up, buying meant winning: every time you bought land you made money. It seemed as easy as that.

The price of development land is a derivative of property prices and it rises (and falls) faster than the value of the finished property. If property rises by 10 per cent, land can

rise by 20 per cent or more, because it is one of the largest
cost inputs into a development. Building costs and professional fees are generally fixed costs moving in line with
inflation; a rise in the value of finished property above the
inflation rate causes a surge in land values. Anglo was very
happy to allow us to determine the price of a tender for land
and we generally kept the level of our bid secret from the
bank until the last minutes of the process. Usually this was
not difficult because we only agreed the figure with minutes
to go. To facilitate this type of bidding, most tenders moved
away from the traditional 10 per cent deposit and towards a
fixed amount. This allowed bidders to sort out the tender
deposit cheque from the bank prior to finalizing the actual
bid figure. I thought 221 was a lucky number and a lot of
my tenders ended with those digits.

With Anglo on our side, we felt we could achieve almost
anything. We considered the bank to be a partner in our
business and the feeling was mutual: the people we dealt
with at Anglo used to ask us regularly, 'When are you
getting an office in the bank?' When we used the big boardroom in Anglo headquarters, where they held the credit
committee meetings, I always sat in the CEO's chair, occupied at actual board meetings by Sean FitzPatrick. 'I want
to get the good karma,' I used to say. We never had to worry
about the money for a deal. Once numbers on the deal
stacked up, Anglo was there – and sometimes Anglo was
there even if the numbers didn't stack up. As we grew
through the boom, we were in the running for most projects
in Dublin. Anything was possible, and we were in the business of trying everything.

Anglo used what they called lending teams. At the top of
a lending team was the associate director, or AD; beneath
him was an ever-rotating cast of managers and sub-managers.

For most of the boom years Kieran Duggan was our AD and this suited everyone just fine. Anglo had six ADs and the man you got – they were all men – set the tone for your whole lending career with the bank. Developers tried hard to get switched to the right AD because the wrong one could cut you out of the market by imposing silly rules and restrictions, effectively giving you a slow 'no'. A good AD just lent the money and managed the credit committee for you. Equity in deals was not really a problem with the right man because equity could always be created with a new asset valuation. Access to funding was a competitive advantage in the market and access to the right AD was the key to this. The managers and sub-managers were there to arrange the details of the deal, but the AD's word was final.

The only people higher up in the bank were God and Jesus – the head of banking and the CEO. From our perspective, the head of banking was the ultimate power in the bank, even higher than the CEO, because Anglo was a lending bank and that was what counted. The CEO was there to keep the share-holders and institutions entertained, but the head of banking was there to lend the money. We always stayed close to him. Over the years we saw a few people in the role; whenever a new person came in, there were consequences.

The 1990s started off with Bill Barrett as head of banking, and he was highly respected by developers. I have never met a grey-haired developer who was not saved at some stage by Bill. At the end of the 1980s he bailed us, and a number of other developers, out with some easy loans and the invitation to get started again. The bad loans were put aside to be paid in the future from new profits, and I think most or all of us eventually made the profits to pay them off. Bill was like a one-man NAMA, though on a much smaller scale, and he had a growing market to play with.

In July 2002 he was replaced by Tom Browne. When Tom took over, 11 September had recently occurred and the dotcom crash had caused a recession in America and most of the world. The Dublin market was in a mini slump partially caused by this and partially by the Bacon Report measures, which disadvantaged investors in order to help homeowners. I think Tom's personal conservatism towards the market was eventually overpowered by the bank's drive to keep lending more money, but we needed Kieran on top of his game to get a few loans past the gatekeeper.

Although the head of banking was God, all of the real action took place within your lending team, and with your AD. You might meet the senior guys a few times a year, generally at high-level congratulatory lunches where we would pat each other on the back.

Our lending team had the time and the budget to give us plenty of special attention, not all of it directly related to the business. If you played golf, they played golf, and they paid to bring you to the best courses. If you liked rugby, they brought you to Lansdowne Road. If you played tennis, which I do, they brought you to Wimbledon.

The credit committee was made up of the ADs, the head of banking and a few others. We heard rumours from other developers of the existence of a head of risk, but none of us worried about him because he had no power in the bank. The ADs all wanted to get their own loans through, so they would not stop each other's. Anything prickly was dealt with in the corridor before the meeting. The meeting was for getting deals approved, and they rarely came back with a no. If a deal looked tricky, the bank would put up the price of the money but lend it anyway.

Apple is cool because Steve Jobs is cool. Ryanair is ruthlessly efficient because Michael O'Leary is ruthlessly efficient.

Oracle is brash and confident because Larry Ellison is brash and confident. Companies become like their founders and that is the story of Anglo. Every senior person in Anglo could trace their lineage at the bank back to their first meeting with the CEO, Sean FitzPatrick. I met Sean a number of times in the bank but I never got to know him at a personal level. Despite that, I feel I do know him because I got to know his bank very well, and his bank got to know a little part of me. Sean hired people like himself. To make it at Anglo, you had to be very quick with the numbers, you had to believe in a project and the people concerned with it, and you had to want to get things done.

In the bank's heyday, borrowing money from Anglo was easy – provided you were an established Anglo client. Once the bank trusted you, money was easily available to play in the duck shoot that was the Irish property market. It was a duck shoot because all you had to do was buy a site with money from the bank, and sell it when the market had risen. There was never an 'if' in this statement because we all expected the market to rise. A falling market was never considered a possibility because the Irish market had never fallen – or so we told ourselves. There had been blips in the past but house-price inflation had always kept these price falls very small and very short. We convinced ourselves and the bank that property was a rock-solid investment with very little risk.

The experience of the UK crash should have prepared me for the risks building up in the Irish market. In truth, we never believed that a large crash was possible. The Irish economy seemed to be powering ahead, and we took property prices to be the side effect of this economic prosperity rather than the cause. Bank adverts always warned, 'Past performance is not an indicator of future returns', but nobody was listening.

We enjoyed having our loyalty to Anglo tested with wonderful offers from other banks. We would always tell Anglo of these approaches, but we remained 100 per cent loyal. It is very important that you trust the bank you borrow from. Irish bank law allows banks to squash you whenever they feel the need, so your relationship with your bank should run deeper than money.

We also wanted to be able to trust our bank not to panic when something went wrong. Problems can and do occur on individual projects, even in an ever-rising market. Some banks would panic if a developer failed to secure planning permission for a project, but Anglo would not. They thought more like developers than bankers. I felt as if I was part of the bank, playing on the same team, and therefore trying to drive all the business I could for the benefit of everyone. We understood, too, that there were penalties for disloyalty. If you left the bank, you left with all your loans and you were never to return. There was a story of a developer who came into Anglo one day to pay off a solid investment property loan, which he had refinanced with another bank. When the bank heard of his plan, they told him to pay off all his loans – good and bad. The cherry-picking of good loans by other banks was not allowed.

Increasingly, as the boom progressed, we did our business in partnerships with other businesspeople: developers, builders and investors. A consequence of this was that we did not always control the banking relationship; but even if Anglo were not involved in a particular project I always kept them up to speed on the details. When I received a loan offer from another bank, I would share the terms with Anglo. Even if I could not steer the partnership business in their direction, I could share the information with them, and receive credit in return to be used in the future when I needed a favour. Anglo was always in my thoughts.

3. Lift-off

You would be excused for thinking that construction is connected to property development, but the link is very subtle. The actual work of getting buildings designed and built is done by architects, engineers, contractors and a whole range of other professionals. Developers are the deal-makers, and once the deal is done we move on to the next.

I learned a long time ago from Paddy to stay away from the site. 'Get somebody good on site and leave them at it,' he told me, probably bouncing me on his knee.

This was fine with me: I preferred to view the projects as the numbers on my computer screen, where they seemed so much neater than the real thing. In my model world, there are costs, rent streams, valuations and cash flows. In the real world, nothing is as tidy and organized. The practical reality of the building site is budgets, compromise and corner-cutting.

I once did the site-management work on a project, attending the weekly project meeting. I hated it. I learned that when the developer is around everybody passes the buck to him, but when the developer is nowhere to be found, decisions get made and the project progresses. When it comes to construction, the right decisions seem to have a habit of being made with or without my input; or, if I'm being more realistic, the wrong decision will get made with or without my input. A building site is a live show and decisions have to be made at every hour of every day. The last thing you want is a developer thinking he's a builder, walking around putting everybody off.

Although the Belfield Office Park build was an enormous project, I never visited the site after the deal was made. The second the ink had dried on the Compaq lease, our minds had moved on to new sites and new opportunities. When you are in a hot market, you have to take the opportunities as they appear. Onwards and upwards was our only thought.

We needed just two things to move on: more money from Anglo, and a valuation for the Belfield Office Park site from Sherry FitzGerald to justify that money. Gordon Gill was head of valuations at Sherry FitzGerald and he was the first man on my list for the valuation. He had a great reputation with the banks and the institutional investors. That is a very important trait for a surveyor. The report, and more importantly the number, needs to be believable. From my perspective, the crucial thing was that the number needed to be high enough to get us some equity. Gordon's number would not be the highest I could get, but it would be the highest that Anglo would accept.

I headed down to the Merrion Row offices of Sherry Fitz-Gerald to get the process started and to give Gordon the squeeze. Gordon is one of the gentlemen of the property business. He has years of experience in every kind of property market and he has seen it all. In spite of that, I thought I could squeeze him a little. My job was to help him see all the potential in Belfield, even though we had not yet finished the construction. I had to get tomorrow's up-side into today's valuation. I enjoyed the process and the metrics of property valuations and I hoped this might help me with Gordon. I'd argue with him using his logic; most other developers probably just argued.

Red-book valuations, as they are called, are generated from a set formula established by the Royal Institute of Chartered Surveyors, and the whole property business has been built up around it.

Rent and yield are the name of the game. The yield on a building represents the annual rent roll as a percentage of the building's value. A building with a rent roll of €1 million, in a market where the prevailing yield was 5 per cent, would be valued at €20 million. A small move in the yield can cause a large move in the building's notional value, and therefore in the debt that can be applied to it. Big values meant more debt and more firepower in the market, and that was what everybody was looking for.

Seemingly everyone I meet in the property business has a Paddy Kelly story. Gordon told me his the moment I sat down in his boardroom to start the meeting.

'I remember Paddy when he first came to Dublin,' Gordon began.

'A country boy up to the city,' I replied jokingly.

'Maybe from the country but not that green,' Gordon said, and he told his story. Paddy had come to Dublin in the late 1960s, having established himself as a successful builder of local-authority housing in the midlands. The eight Kelly brothers – C. Kelly and Sons – had done well, building houses for the government, but Paddy wanted more. He had worked out that buying the land, getting planning permission, and building houses on spec was a lot more profitable than contracting for the local authority. On arriving in Dublin, he had gone to see P.V. Doyle, who was one of the men leading the charge to develop property in Dublin at the time. His first hotel was the Montrose, which he opened in 1964, and he went on to develop a string of hotels, which became the Jurys Doyle Group. He had also made a lot of money on a property development in Churchtown.

'What's the secret?' Paddy asked PV.

'Own and keep the land and the buildings,' was PV's answer. Up to this point, Paddy had been building houses on contract. Acting as a developer was a totally different style of business. While the advice to buy and hold property was common, the source of the advice was what inspired Paddy. He had sought out P.V. Doyle because he inspired him.

One of his first deals on arriving in Dublin was to buy land on the Castletown House estate in County Kildare. To get this deal over the line with the bank Paddy needed a valuation. A very young Gordon Gill was sent out from Dublin to meet him on the site. As Gordon told the story, he had pulled up in his banger of a car to be met by a twenty-six-year-old Paddy in his new Rolls-Royce. Gordon got into the car, careful not to damage the leather. As he sucked in his first lungful of British luxury, Paddy proceeded to pull off and drive the car over the fields so that they could see the entire site. To be fair to Paddy, four-wheel-drive jeeps had not yet been introduced into Ireland, and he did not have another car apart from the Rolls in which to take Gordon on the tour. Gordon left that first meeting, remembering the car, the luxury, the smell, the leather, but nothing of the site. Paddy got the right number for the valuation and the deal went ahead.

My first meeting with Gordon about Belfield was in a much more conventional setting. His office was on Merrion Row and it connected with a Georgian building on Ely Place, where the commercial end of Sherry FitzGerald was located. Gordon is a numbers guy in the old sense. Rent, ERV (estimated rental value) and yield are his tools, and out of these three numbers my Belfield valuation would emerge. The only fixed number that I could not argue about with Gordon was the rent, because the leases had already been signed. Everything else was up for grabs.

Pots of coffee were brought into the boardroom and the game began. I had brought along a new laptop, preloaded with all the various permutations of the figures for the valuation. I had a positive for every negative that Gordon could throw at me – and perhaps I was hoping that Gordon would still be a little blinded by that long-ago day with Paddy in the Rolls at Castletown House.

Banks believe valuers, which always amazes me because valuers don't buy buildings. Some time ago, a system evolved whereby a valuer's word was absolute, and a valuation was almost as good as money in the bank. Valuation figures could be swapped for real money less a discount of about 20 per cent: we'd be able to borrow 80 per cent of whatever figure I could squeeze out of Gordon. An extra million in the valuation would be like Gordon writing me a cheque for £800,000.

The Compaq rent deal had been agreed at about £12 per square foot, but the most recent deals in Belfield had been increased to about £15 per square foot. Gordon and I agreed that £12 was now historic and we could use £15 as the ERV in our valuation. Rental levels were rising very quickly during the boom and an increase in the ERV of a building was regularly used to justify an increased valuation. The first rent review of the Compaq lease was five years away, and by using this higher ERV we were bringing the future rental increases on the building into today's valuation.

The final battle came down to yield. This is the most important figure to be agreed for a property valuation, and in principle it comes from the market: the yields of comparable rental properties generally dictate the yield estimate that is used in a valuation. There is a lot to argue over on this battleground – no two properties are identical, and firm information about rents and values of other properties is very hard to come by – and I was not going to give in easily. The difference between a five per cent and a 5.5 per cent yield would be about £6,000,000 in the valuation of Belfield, so this one meant a lot to me. To get a grip on yields we were all reading the newspapers, trying to get a feel for the market, but the media never got it totally right. We did not like referring to foreign market property yields because they always tended to be higher than the Irish market.

Gordon tended to value property about 10 per cent below the probable sale price, or so I told him. He was a great lagging indicator of the true market.

'I'll buy any building for the price you value it at,' I told him. 'It will be like buying pounds for 90p.'

Gordon had heard it all before, but I think I might have brought a new passion and logic to the debate. Most valuers were left alone to do their work, but Gordon and I had about six meetings on the Belfield valuation. In the end, I gave a little ground on the yield because I had got full value for the imaginary rent with the ERV. The battle over yield had left me a little shy of my target number, but there was a silver lining. Yields were falling all over Dublin as investors were paying more and more for buildings. We could do the whole valuation again next year using higher ERV rents and lower yields. In the end, a valuation is only a snapshot in time, and it could be revisited in the future, if we needed to gear up on the building again with the bank.

'I'll be back next year to push this a little with the yield,' I told Gordon.

'I'd expect nothing less of you, Simon,' he replied, resigned to do battle again in the near future.

I was pretty happy with the final number, which was about £60 million. It was not a bad result for a few guys who had got together and bought some land for £3.25 million. The completed cost of the entire development was less than £30 million, including the original land cost, so we now had the equity and firepower to go again. We had made a paper profit of about £30 million and Anglo could give us an equity release loan of about £20 million from that. With the Belfield deal, our biggest to date, we felt we had arrived.

'The auction is at three,' I shouted to Paddy, who was in the next room mulling over some drawings. There was an old 1960s office building up for sale on Hatch Street that day and we were having a look at the numbers.

'What extra space can we get on it?' Paddy asked.

I brought my laptop into the boardroom. Since the Belfield deal we had moved out of the home office on Shrewsbury Road and into a Georgian building in Baggot Street. Our new landlord was a property developer called Paddy Kelly: there were two property developers in Ireland called Paddy Kelly, and that caused no end of confusion for some people. My Paddy Kelly was sometimes referred to as 'posh Paddy' – I think this dated back to the Rolls-Royce years.

'We're adding about twenty thousand square feet to the back of the building,' I replied.

HKR Architects had had a quick look at the site for us, and our plan was to refit the current building, adding some space to the back and maybe an additional floor on top. We had teamed up with John Flynn on this one. It was our first auction since Belfield and we were feeling pretty good about our chances.

I had set up a model for this kind of development, so we could make quick decisions on the value and potential of the site. Paddy and I could have a set of numbers ready in less than five minutes for any project. We only really started to look at the Hatch Street project on the day of the auction, which was to be held at three p.m. Paddy put a call in to Anglo to inform them that we'd be bidding; he was assured that the deposit money would not be a problem. At this stage of a deal, all that counted was the deposit money. We could worry about the balance another day. The memories of the first deals, when we had no money and had to scramble for loans, were still fresh in my mind, and it was great not to have to worry about that any more.

The building we were to bid on was beside the Deloitte & Touche offices in the heart of professional Dublin. In its current state, it was a sorry picture, with outdated windows and an ugly façade. It was basically a shell that we could refurbish and add to. We left the office with confidence high and cheque book at the ready. If we won the bid and had to write a cheque for 10 per cent, Anglo would transfer the funds to meet the cheque. I had set up the computer model backwards to help us on this bid. Once you entered a building area and land value into the model, it would generate the rent per square foot that was needed to make the project viable. That meant I could adjust the land-value figure as the bids moved upwards, and we could see the rent per square foot that would be required at this level of bidding.

We met John Flynn in a coffee shop near the auction room beforehand to give him the rundown on our approach. John and Paddy have been partners on a continual basis since they met in the early 1970s. As Paddy told the story, John was in trouble with his banks and needed some help and advice. C. Kelly and Sons had successfully gone through an insolvency process. The company had come out the other side and the creditors had been fully paid. Paddy therefore had the experience to advise others who got into similar trouble. I was born around the same time, and John, a kind man with a gentle manner, became my godfather.

I brought John through the figures and our assumptions over coffee and scones. We all agreed that the location was good and that, with rents rising, we could afford to be bullish.

We left the café with an air of excitement, expecting to spend some money. A competitive auction for a desirable property has the adrenalin, drama and competing egos of a sporting event, and winning gives you a great buzz. There is no agreed method to a successful auction strategy. Some people like to skulk in the corners, hoping to be ignored and then pouncing at the end with a killer bid. Some like to send in a lawyer to do their bidding, staying in touch on the phone. We preferred the full-frontal attack. Our strategy was to let everybody know that we were in the room and that we were there to buy.

The market knew we had done well in Belfield, which had been ranked as the deal of the year in the *Irish Times*. Paddy's planning powers had reached mystic levels, so people would presume that we had another angle on this one.

'Scare them into not bidding,' was the plan.

We made a point of arriving a little late. The room was packed. We took seats in the centre of the room and puffed out our chests as if to say, 'Stay away. We're here to buy today.' The auction room murmured with excitement as the doors were closed and we settled down.

We had decided to let John do the bidding for our consortium. We had agreed that we'd bid up to about £6 million, and confer after the price reached that level. The top table in the room where the vendor's team sat began to fill with the usual gathering of serious-looking solicitors and advisers. They had to look serious to create the right atmosphere, but I could see they were happy. There was money in the room and it was going to fly.

The auctioneer took to his feet and started the bidding. 'What we have today here, ladies and gentlemen, is a unique opportunity to buy a prime office building in Dublin 2.' I kept thinking about the numbers in my head: £18 per square foot was what we had planned as our bidding rent, which had driven out the land value and our bid amount of about £6 million. I tried to apply logic to the situation, but we were basically winging it. Logic alone did not get land bought.

His sales pitch concluded, the auctioneer opened the bidding. After a few moments' silence, a bid was made. It wasn't a familiar face but they rarely were – not many developers adopted our direct approach.

We countered the initial bid. In no time, the bidding had gone well over our notional £6 million ceiling. John was keen to keep going higher, but we were now in uncomfortable territory. My numbers were history and the bidding was being driven up by emotion. This was about ownership and success. We wanted to own the building, but it seemed as though somebody else wanted it more. By my calculations, the required rent was being driven to over £20 per square foot, and that was crazy in my view.

At the end we pulled back – the price was too rich even for us. The other bidder was obviously working on different assumptions. The market had reached a new level and the whole room knew it. Half of those in it were only there to watch, but they went back to their offices knowing one thing: this market was going higher.

Walking down the street afterwards, we discussed the implications. We were in shock because we had gone to the auction to buy, which normally meant success. We had never before been outbid when we'd really wanted the deal. This time we had gone well over our limit to try to win, but it had not been enough.

'Land is now worth more than the buildings on it,' John said, as we rounded the corner.

This was a very significant observation. Up to that point we had looked at central Dublin as a series of buildings that seemed to be fixed for all eternity. Office buildings were not being torn down regularly to make way for new development, but this would start to happen. Now we looked upon Dublin as a flat map full of opportunities, with the buildings ready to be torn down. Land was the name of the game and Dublin was full of it. The buildings no longer mattered.

Everything had to be recalibrated. All our assumptions had to change.

'We need to try again in the IFSC,' Paddy said, one afternoon in the office in November 1997. We were still flush from our success in Belfield and looking to expand.

Along with two of our colleagues from the Tallaght consortium, John Walsh and John McCabe, we had tendered and won the right to develop offices above the train platform at Connolly Station. The land was owned by CIE and not by the Dublin Docklands Development Authority (DDDA). It was not officially an IFSC site, but once the development was complete it would in effect form part of the IFSC. The site was within the DDDA planning area, so we would be able to use the Section 25 planning process and fast-track the application.

Section 25 planning certificates could be granted by the DDDA where the proposed scheme complied with the master plan for the area. A certificate exempted you from the need to secure planning permission from Dublin City Council. This was very popular with developers because it eliminated the risk of a planning refusal, or of major delays arising from third-party objections and appeals.

Winning the bid was great news because it was a sign of our acceptance into the establishment core of Irish property developers. The IFSC was the holy grail, where you played with the big boys. Phase 1 of the development of the IFSC was a joint venture between Hardwicke Developments, the winner of the auction for Hatch Street, and British Land. The buildings were of a very high quality and the tenants even better: Irish and international financial institutions. All the right players chose the IFSC as their pitch and wanted in. The suburbs were okay for the odd deal, but downtown was where we wanted our business to grow.

After the initial euphoria of winning the tender with CIE, we discovered a cost flaw in our figures, which generated a loss in our financial models. We had put too low a figure on the ancillary works involved in building above a working railway station, and we had to withdraw from the tender with no small amount of embarrassment. We tried again with a tender for an office block at the corner of Manor Street but failed once more.

In September 1998 a new tender was announced for a hotel, and this provided us with a fresh opportunity to get back in the frame as developers in the IFSC.

'We'll need a totally new team for this one,' I said to Paddy, at a meeting at his home on Shrewsbury Road. We had failed twice with the IFSC, and I felt that new people would help our chances.

Paddy agreed, and suggested that we link up with the McCormacks, our old sparring partners in Tallaght. Paddy had a lot of time and respect for John McCormack, and his company had experience as consultants in the IFSC on a number of projects. Paddy and John had repaired the damage to their relationship after Tallaght and had decided to look at a few projects on a fifty-fifty basis.

Alan McCormack was John's youngest son and he had recently left his job as an investment banker in London to return to Dublin and join the family business. The boom was sucking in new people and energy all the time. Alan had lived like an investment banker in London, and he brought this glamour to Dublin by immediately buying a Georgian house as his new residence and the office for the family business. This brought a new meaning to 'living over the shop'.

My first meeting with Alan was in the conservatory at Paddy's house on a sunny afternoon. I'm pretty sure it didn't come about by chance. Alan turned up in a black suit and stepped out of a vintage red Mercedes convertible. He casually told me that he owned three vintage Mercedes. Our only common ground was that I had bought an old Porsche 911, and Paddy tried to bring us together over our interest in cars. He really wanted us to click as development partners. My battered old Porsche, however, did not compare to the vintage Mercs.

Sitting in the sun that day, Alan talked of London and banking and getting involved with some deals in Dublin. He spoke a more sophisticated language than the one we were used to. He used terms from the world of investment banking, like 'risk' and 'margin', and brought a more scientific air to the business of development. I presumed he knew what he was at, so we started working together.

Alan and I arranged to meet up again at the McCormacks' offices in Fitzwilliam Square to discuss the hotel tender we were looking at in the IFSC. You never got a lot of information from the McCormacks – their style is to look for your view and then to ponder – and Alan was no exception.

'What do you think about this one?' he asked.

I told him I thought it looked great. We all knew that the IFSC was now a very well-established office location. We thought a good business hotel would work well in that location. A lot of people did not share this view, however: they saw the IFSC as completely detached from Dublin and

believed that tourists wouldn't stay there. We had little time
for these negatives and pushed ahead.

'I think we should stick with a team that the DDDA like,'
Alan said.

'Agreed,' was my swift response. The DDDA was the
government, and the government likes nicely named professional firms with long titles. We discussed the various
professionals who would appeal to the conservative nature
of the DDDA board. Tenders of this nature were not only
decided on price. You had also to win in categories such as
design and deliverability and, in this case, hotel quality.
With these things in mind, we brought in Scott Tallon
Walker as architects for the bid. Scott's, as we call them,
have been at the vanguard of office and commercial design
in Ireland since the 1960s and the founders are gods of architecture. Scott's had also built a number of other office
buildings in the IFSC so the DDDA were sure to be happy
with them. We brought in engineers and other professionals similarly calculated to please the authority. On top of
this professional team we lined up A & L Goodbody as
lawyers and Anglo as bankers.

It was a dream team of establishment professionals, all of
whom were very happy to join Alan and me: experience
lining up behind two young developers.

Tendering for DDDA land required you to pull together
a large amount of documentation and information because
your bid had to cover both price and the concept of the
project.

Alan and I agreed that he'd look after the bank and the
lawyers, and I'd look after the design. This seemed a fair split
of the tasks.

We had some knowledge of hotels, having recently acquired
one on Leeson Street called Stephen's Hall from the Aer

Lingus pilots' pension fund. This purchase had led us to a second hotel at Morrison's Island in Cork, which was owned by the same fund. Tax breaks were central to our move into the hotel business. We were building up a portfolio of profitable office properties and we could use the hotels to ensure that this income was tax-free.

In the Cork purchase, we narrowly beat a bid from a UK firm called Friendly Hotels plc. Paddy liked the look of the company and its management. Ever aware of the need for tenants in our buildings, we set up Choice Hotels Ireland, as a joint venture with Friendly, to build and run hotels in Ireland, with Frankie Whelan as our CEO. It was a fifty-fifty arrangement with Peter Cashman representing Friendly Hotels' stake in the deal.

Very little hotel development had happened in Dublin in the recent past, so a strong joint venture with a UK plc was a useful calling card on the tender. However, Friendly was not exactly at the quality end of the hotel business in the UK, and that was a hurdle we needed to overcome for this tender.

In the UK, Friendly traded under the hotel brands Quality and Comfort, which occupied the two- and three-star markets. They were part owned by a large American company called Choice Hotels (we named our Irish company after the US parent). We noticed on the American website that they had a four-star brand called Clarion and decided that this would be our brand for the hotel on the north quays.

With that settled, we needed to push on with the design. Scott's had never designed a hotel before so I put them together with our hotel consultant to start the work. We needed to know how big a hotel we could get on the site in order to work out what we could pay for the deal. We had to hold Scott's hand a little through this process, but in the end we came up with a nice 150-bedroom hotel sitting on top of a typical ground-floor pub and restaurant. We toyed with having a nightclub in the basement but settled on a gym.

While I was working up the design for the hotel and dealing with the tenant company, Alan was crunching the numbers. We had to build to a turnkey standard – everything down to the cups and spoons – and that was pushing up the costs. It was a far cry from the office developments we were used to. In a standard office scheme, the developer would finish the building to a shell and core standard, leaving most of it as bare concrete. Ronnie Tallon, one of the founders of the architectural firm, took a very keen interest in the project, right down to the details of the furniture, and he pushed us along a stylish – and expensive – road. It was lining up to be one of the most expensive hotels ever built in Dublin, and the hoteliers were worried about making it pay.

The moment of truth with Scott's came when Ronnie Tallon asked me about the art budget for the project. I told him honestly that I had not considered one. A shadow passed over his face as he looked down his nose at me.

'I personally bought all the art for Bank of Ireland's headquarters, and they have made a tidy sum,' he said.

'Ronnie, we can't afford that,' I said. 'We have about a hundred pounds per room in mind.'

The meeting moved on, but I had the impression that Ronnie lost interest in our hotel at that stage. I did not see him at any more design meetings.

We had some leeway in the budget because of the extremely generous tax breaks on offer in the IFSC. As in Tallaght in the early years, tenants were able to claim double rent allowance. In addition to this, the hotel's owners would be able to claim capital allowances over seven years.

I struck a target rent on the hotel of £2 million per annum, which indicated a capital value of about £30 million based on a yield of about 6.15 per cent when costs were included. This figure was roughly equal to the total building cost of the hotel, so it looked as if we couldn't make a profit on the deal. We were really building the hotel to keep it as a long-term asset, and for the tax breaks that we could keep or sell. But we needed to find a new angle to make the figures work a bit better.

'Let's bring in Pierse and Derek Quinlan,' Alan suggested. That made sense to me. A large section of the qualification element for DDDA tenders is a financial questionnaire involving turnover and profitability. It was written by accountants who only considered limited companies capable of making bids for development sites. To qualify you had to provide three years' audited accounts with turnover in excess of £50 million per annum. Alan and I had been trying to work up these figures from our private property interests, but we couldn't fit into the criteria. A large contractor with high turnover would solve this problem, so we settled on Pierse. We would add their balance sheet to the project.

To squeeze every last drop out of our bid we would need to sell on to investors at the highest price possible the tax breaks that would come with the hotel, and Derek Quinlan was just the man to do this. Derek was a former Revenue inspector who had built up a successful practice selling tax-based property investments to high-net-worth investors. It was normal practice for us to separate the property asset from its tax allowances and sell the tax breaks to investors who needed them. In effect, they were buying pure tax allowances, and had no real ownership or interest in the hotel. In this separated form, hotel tax breaks were basically a straight subsidy to the hotel industry. We needed that subsidy to be able to make our bid stack up in the IFSC.

The bid pack was looking good. Alan had lined up the required letter of support from Anglo Irish Bank, and we had a great-looking hotel from Scott's. One problem remained.

'Have you looked at the Clarion website?' Niall McCormack asked me.

I had. It didn't look great. We had been looking for supporting information on the Clarion brand to add to our tender pack. The hotel in the USA seemed like the kind of place where you might end your days. Tired, old and trashy.

'All American hotels are like that,' was my rationalization. We needed Friendly Hotels and the Clarion brand because they were providing a £2 million guarantee on the lease and this was a cornerstone to the banking package.

Eventually I found a nice image of a four-star Clarion in Norway. We built the entire hotel brand pack around the Scott Tallon Walker interior design boards and the one Clarion Hotel in the world that looked like the sort of thing we were aiming for. None of us had seen a Clarion in person, and we certainly had not gone to Norway, but we took a chance and ran with it anyway.

In late November 1998, on the final day of the bid, I called over to Alan's office in Fitzwilliam Square to sign the tender documents. 'That's a great-looking pack,' I said, as Alan brought in the weighty file for me to sign.

'It's the way they like it,' was Alan's response. At eleven fifteen I signed off the offer package with a land price of £7 million, and we sent it on its way to the DDDA offices.

The team had pulled together fantastically and we were confident that our bid would be difficult to beat.

Within days, we had received word back that the deal was

on – but there was one query from the DDDA: 'Who the hell are Clarion?'

'They're a great company. You should see their hotel in Norway – six-star!' was our response.

We won the tender. That little hotel on the docks opened up the whole of the IFSC to our hungry eyes.

4. Cruise Control

'How's the fund going, guys?' Paddy asked, as he popped his head around the door. I was with Steve McNeill, a boyhood friend, in the office we used for the small investment fund we set up in 1999 to speculate on listed companies and currencies coinciding with the launch of the euro.

'Great, Paddy,' we replied in unison.

'Just leaving this Warren Buffett book for you guys to read,' Paddy said. 'If you can keep up with him, I'll be impressed.'

Paddy had little time for our trading business, but I loved it. Buying and selling things at the push of a button was the perfect business for me. I loved the technology but I also loved the absence of people: you could buy a share or sell an option and nobody else had to know anything about it. No need for a breakfast meeting, just nerves of steel and a steady head.

My interest in the stock market had been sparked by my grandfather Joe, who was involved with a few listed companies. My mum had done really well with Conroy Resources, buying their shares on a tip at less than 50p and selling out at over £7 near the peak. As a family we had watched the rise and had a nice holiday in Disney World out of the trade. I liked the idea of easy money and this seemed a good way to go about getting it.

Steve and I had opened an account with IG Index in the mid-1990s and we had built up a bit of experience in trading complex instruments. IG Index was initially set up as a spread-trading business but it soon expanded into a full consumer-fronted derivatives business. Through IG, we were able to speculate on all of the major futures and options exchanges. Everything from share prices to potato prices can be traded. All of these exchanges are restricted to experienced investors, and IG gave us access to these markets.

We had played around a bit at first – acting as classic cannon fodder for the market – and after a few big losses we had managed to get back to zero.

'This is a mug's game,' Steve said one day. 'We need a market where we know something special.' That was when we started thinking about Anglo shares. We set up a spreadsheet detailing the bank's profits from the early 1990s up to about 1998, and the results were startling. At the time we were trading, a lot of tech stocks and the world markets were booming, based on tech, the Internet and growth stories. But even compared to the booming tech stocks, Anglo's numbers jumped off the page. The bank had been growing at more than 30 per cent per annum for a number of years, yet the stock price seemed to be stuck. That meant only one thing to us: it was about to explode.

We got on the telephone to our broker at IG and put in our first order for 10,000 shares at 70p per share. The stock later split one share for every share in existence, so our effective entry price was 35p. We did not purchase the shares directly, but took a derivative position in their value via contracts for difference (CFDs). Owning a CFD is not the same as owning shares in a company. Your name does not appear on the share register and you do not have any shareholders' rights. You are merely betting on the future movement of the share price, and the CFD allows you to do this with plenty of leverage. Your paper profits are recognized by the trading house as equity, and you can spend this equity on further investment.

Because Anglo was still so obscure, we had to take the position on a margin of 33 per cent – meaning we had to deposit 33 per cent of the value of the position as collateral with IG. This was high compared to larger and more heavily traded companies, where we only needed 10 per cent margin. The initial 10,000 shares in Anglo would have cost £7,000 and IG required a margin of £2,310.

I became an evangelist for the stock, and Steve and I kept buying more shares. We tried repeating the Anglo magic with other bank shares, and thought we had found a similar bank in Australia, but on further inspection it was not the same. Nothing was the same as the little Irish bank up the road that seemed to have invented a magic formula for making money.

Stock-pickers spend years looking for a great undiscovered share. It's a bit like gold mining. You go down the pit every day looking for gold and everybody thinks you're crazy. In Anglo, Ireland had one of the most dynamic and successful growth stories, and nobody knew about it. We had found our little gold mine.

Pretty soon, we were long on Anglo shares with all the money our little fund had. Anglo-watch was the fund's daily activity. We traded a lot because we could not get any income by just sitting on the share. The trading pattern in Anglo became familiar to us: the price always went up in advance of the year-end, so we always sold then and bought later in the cycle, when the shares tended to fall off a bit.

Eventually the Anglo secret got out. International institutions were buying the share as a supercharged way of getting exposure to a supercharged economy, and punters were trading the cycles like we were. Anglo's daily volume rose to challenge the bellwether stocks on the Irish market.

Our little position in Anglo was to grow to over €1 million with no extra cash invested apart from that initial £2,310.

We were able to use our paper profits from Anglo shares to buy more Anglo shares: every time we made £1,000 on our existing shares, we could buy £3,000 worth of new shares. This was exactly the kind of equity growth that property developers were able to generate through the boom from very limited amounts of initial capital. As with CFDs, the profits from one deal or trade could be rolled as equity into the next deal.

A great thing about the leverage we got with IG in the CFD market was that there was no need to ask anyone for the money. It was available for everybody who signed up to trade. This was one difference between the workings of CFD and development leverage. Another was that IG would close out your position without hesitation if you were heading for a loss. In property, there was no similar mechanism because the true value of property is much more difficult to determine than the price of a share, and because it is very difficult to close out a position in the property market.

I really liked the CFD world because at a push of a button you could convert all your paper profits on speculative positions into real money. There were days when we felt Anglo shares had run too far too fast so we sold out. In property development, that sort of flexibility, and freedom, just didn't exist,

'Why bother being in business? Let's just buy Anglo shares,' I said to Paddy a few times. What most impressed me was the bank's ability to grow its loan book every year. Loans meant profits, because the market never considered the concept of loans not being repaid. Every loan generated fees and interest and the bank's balance sheet continued to grow.

Banking in a booming market is like shooting fish in a barrel. A bank will have 60 to 70 per cent of its profits lined up every year in advance from interest on existing loans.

Taking guys like me to smart breakfasts in the Shelbourne was an easy way of generating the new additional loans and profits. That's why I had a lot of breakfasts. Of course we could pay the money back because we were buying great assets, and Ireland was booming.

'I'm a shareholder now, so be nice,' I'd tell Anglo bankers in meetings, smirking with pride.

I met only one person during the boom years who seriously challenged my view of Anglo Irish Bank. In 2003 I flew to London for my friend Foxy's thirtieth birthday party. I loved going out for a few beers with old school friends, and my gang from St Andrew's College had stayed pretty close. St Andrew's produces interesting and diverse people, so I was the only developer at the party.

We gathered in a pub where Foxy worked as chef and we had taken over the place for the whole night to celebrate his birthday. After the initial polite hellos, and the mixing of the old friends with the new London friends, the beer began to flow and so did the chatter.

When the party was winding down and the bodies were being moved off the floor and into the waiting taxis, I sat down in the corner with a great friend called Roger Duggan. Roger and I had gone to school together from the age of eight so we knew each other pretty well. While I was becoming a speculative property developer, he was working with a German bank in the IFSC. He and I began to talk Anglo, and he had some pretty strong views.

'They're a shower of spoofers,' Roger said. 'They lend money to anybody and their clients are shit.'

'I know those clients and I'm one of them,' I replied. We took the conversation into the taxi and kept at it, Roger attacking my bank and all it stood for, and me defending it with all my drink-induced powers. I was not going to let this go.

Back and forth we went until we got back to the shabby hotel where we were staying. There was no fancy residents' bar, but we managed to get the night porter to give us a few more bottles of beer, having promised him we would be quiet and not cause trouble. He knew there was more chance of us falling asleep.

Despite the beer, we were able to argue with logic.

'Their balance sheet is full of shit,' Roger said.

'The balance sheet doesn't put a value on their client loyalty,' I parried.

'The clients are all Paddies with no money,' he replied.

We gave up at about five in the morning and I staggered to bed.

Roger was the first person I had met who had questioned Anglo's business model. He was smart like me, I thought, and a banker to boot. Could he not see the magic? I chalked the discussion up to sour grapes and establishment jealousy. Roger, I convinced myself, was an establishment man, and therefore out to talk down the new kid on the block.

Anglo loved golf, and they really loved golf with good clients. I enjoyed the game in my thoughts, but rarely in reality, and I only played a little. Those bank outings were not really my style. Steve and I used to play at the Stepaside public course, and this was a great place to discuss the Anglo share price and our stock-trading strategy. We would ring up our broker in between holes to check our positions. Now, this was my idea of golf: having a laugh with your mate and not really counting the score, with a little bit of work thrown in. Prancing around the K Club worrying if you'd parked in the right car space, or if you were wearing the right clothes, was a different game altogether. On the few occasions that I was coaxed out to a bank day or charity game, I usually drove home early cursing the sport. I always regretted saying yes to corporate golf, generally wishing I had given the day over to a real sport or even to work. 'When you're all playing golf, I can't get into credit committee,' was my complaint to Anglo.

There was, however, one golf day I never missed: the annual Anglo classic at Druids Glen. Every year I would turn up to collect my golf goody-bag and hack my way around the immaculate course. I always asked to play on the worst team, because I never wanted to have to take the game seriously. Winning at golf seemed to be the basis for a lot of developers' lives. To them, their score in golf was nearly as important as the money in the deals. 'Let's play for fun,' was always my opening gambit on the first tee when I met my playing partners. 'We're not going to win so we'll enjoy the walk.'

'Simon Kelly, twenty-four, So-and-so, twenty-four, So-and-so, twenty-two, and So-and-so, twenty-three' – when you heard those kinds of handicaps read out at the first tee you knew that you would enjoy the day. The problem with golf was that one good shot – which generally happens during the closing holes, the shot where you feel a clean connection and hear the beautiful 'ping' from the club head – was enough to make you want to come back. One hundred rubbish shots, followed by one or two sweet connections, and you had yourself convinced that this might be your game.

If you want to borrow money from a bank during the summer, your best chance for a soft hearing is on the golf course.

'Do you want to meet on Tuesday to discuss the loan?' I would ask the bank.

'Can't,' was often the answer. 'Unless you want to play golf?'

'No, thanks. I'll wait till you get back to work,' was my answer to that one.

I wasn't a member of a club, yet I could play for free twice a week through the summer if I wanted to: Anglo on a Tuesday followed by Bank of Ireland on a Thursday.

The Anglo day at Druids Glen was seventy-one red-faced builders and bankers dressed to the nines believing they were golf gods, and me. In 2003 we were playing the course a week after a major tournament, and rumour ran that it was going to be in amazing condition, which to me meant that it would be a bastard to play. Druids, that year, was going to eat balls. I made a mental note to get some extras off the bank at registration.

I drove off to Druids with the golf clubs resting on the passenger seat of the Porsche. The old 911 was not really designed for the developer-golfer type because the boot has no room for clubs – or for builder's gear. I pulled into the car park and squeezed between two monstrous S Class Mercedes – the standard form of transport for builder/developers.

'Hiya, lads,' I shouted to two of the younger Anglo loan executives, as I lugged my gear up to the clubhouse. Some of the junior Anglo people were asked along to the golf day, but they didn't get to play. They were there to network and keep the clients happy.

The great thing about the Anglo golf day was that you needed to bring very little with you. Whatever you didn't have, they would get for you. The event generally provided my golf clothes for the year. The previous year, 2002, had been a good one for the bank, and they seemed to be splashing the cash at the event. I suppose that, like the profit figures, every year's golf classic needed to be more impressive than the last. We were all really there to congratulate each other on our great success and intelligence.

Breakfast was available from a small mobile catering unit but I skipped past it, heading for the registration desk to sign in and collect my goodies. A travel bag, plenty of balls and a golf top were that year's haul, along with a bag of food and sun cream. Then I walked out towards the first tee to meet my playing partners. As requested, I had been put on the degenerates' team.

The first at Druids is a pretty public tee box, and the first tee box is a lonely place in golf for all bad players. 'Driver or wood?' is the question rushing through every duffer's mind. We know that the answer is wood, but the ego calls for the driver. All eyes are on the hitter, and there is a warped hope among the onlooking players that they'll see a few hilarious shots. The first drive and the last shot on to the eighteenth green were the key shots of the day for me. Get off the box without making a mess of it, and hit a nice approach into the eighteenth where everybody will be watching. Everything else could be fun, I hoped.

I addressed the ball, and hit a sweet one. That's not to say I split the fairway, but at least I was well past the ladies' tee box, and vaguely in the direction of the green. One of my playing partners topped his shot, which dribbled near the ladies' tee box. We all had somebody to feel sorry for, which suited me fine. Anybody but me.

I hacked my way around the course, eating through my supply of golf balls and swearing to myself. Druids looked beautiful but it was one tough lady. My wonder moment came at the twelfth. Anglo had provided Des Smyth, an old pro who had represented Europe in the Ryder Cup, to hit a tee shot with all the players on this famous hole, a beautiful par three. The tee box overlooks a river and a perfect green.

As you stand over your ball, you can visualize the shots of the greats, the ball fizzing through the air, landing on the green and rolling towards the pin.

'What's the handicap, boys?' Des asked us, as we all walked on to the tee box.

'Twenty-four, twenty-two, twenty-two, twenty-four . . .' I could see Des calculating how many balls would hit the river.

He hit off first and landed his ball within two feet of the pin.

'How's that, then?' he asked us, grinning from ear to ear.

We shuffled a little. He had hit a beauty; we just hoped to avoid the embarrassment of the river. One of my playing partners hit the green, another the river. Then it was my turn. I stepped up to the tee box in third place after my playing partners had done well. One on the green, and one short by the river. Nothing to write home about but all the balls were dry.

Gripping my eight-iron, I visualized myself hitting a great shot. I didn't use a tee because I wanted a clean connection. I pulled back my swing and launched down towards the ball with full power.

The connection felt really good. I kept my head down and glanced up only when the ball was well on its way.

It looked great. I stood proudly on the tee box and followed the ball, trying to look as though this was a normal shot for me. The ball landed on the green a foot from the hole, closer to the pin than the amazing shot of Des Smyth. It stopped dead, which made it look even better.

'What's your handicap?' Des asked me again, with shock on his face.

'Twenty-four,' I told him, as I gathered up my clubs and headed down to the green.

The other holes didn't matter now because I had the shot to brag about. Halfway around the course I grabbed a look at my phone to see if I had any text messages. There was one from the office.

Smithfield planning permission granted.

The chat among the developers was that Smithfield – an enormous cobbled square in the north inner city surrounded by fruit-and-veg wholesalers, scrapyards and greasy spoons – was the next Temple Bar. We were all sniffing around, looking for some action. Dublin City Council had established the Historic Area Rejuvenation Project (HARP) in 1996 to revitalize this part of Dublin.

There was a scrapyard on the square, owned by a man called Charlie Duffy. One day in 2002 Paddy and John Flynn went to see him. We had hardly discussed the site in the office so I didn't think much would come of the meeting.

Later in the day, Paddy rang. 'We've bought it,' he said.

'Bought what?' I asked him.

'Smithfield,' he answered. 'We've done the deal. Take a note of this . . .' He started to give me the details. I opened a new Word document on my laptop and took notes.

We had agreed to pay €8 million for the scrapyard site, which was the asking price. Charlie would not take a penny less. Of this, we would pay €1 million up front. The remaining €7 million would be paid two years later, an arrangement that gave us time to get the planning permission and finance arranged. Duffy struck a hard bargain and the agreement had a few frills. The first condition was that we would sign the contract the next day, and the second was that we would guarantee that his tax rate would not exceed 20 per cent. Capital gains tax at the time was set at 20 per cent for residential development land, but there was a risk that this deal might be taxed at a higher level due to the mixed nature of the development we planned. We were agreeing to pay the difference if the government chose to apply a higher rate. Our willingness to take this risk won us the deal over the competition.

'Where will we get the million?' I asked.

'Kieran in Anglo is sorting it for us,' was Paddy's predictable answer.

We were hoping to develop the entire west side of Smithfield, and the Duffy lands made up about half of the relevant area. Under the HARP designation, the city could acquire the land under a compulsory purchase order (CPO) for the purpose of redevelopment in the event that the owners could not work together. The government will often put a CPO on a piece of land, like Smithfield, where it hopes to promote new development but where it feels that the existing property owners cannot come together to create a commercial deal. The CPO forces the owners to reach agreement with each other, or a third party like ourselves. Selling to the state under a CPO was the worst possible result.

The CPO process does not deliver a high price for land and the payment terms are very uncertain. In Smithfield, the threat of a CPO pushed all the other landowners into our arms.

Smithfield had been a big deal in Dublin since Terry Devey paid Hugh O'Regan a large premium for his site there, making Hugh a millionaire overnight. Terry had put Smithfield on the map, building apartments, offices and a hotel on the east side of the square, and refurbishing the Jameson Tower as a tourist attraction. He had shown ambition for the area and its tourism potential; now we were hoping to take it to a new level with a large mixed-use development consisting of shops, offices and apartments. Paddy was influenced by similar developments he had seen around the world, and we planned to bring some of this world vision to Smithfield.

The site Paddy had part-bought totalled 4.25 acres, which made it a very large piece of Dublin. Now the deal had been struck we immediately got stuck into the details and the team. It was always our approach to seek partners for every deal. We did this to spread the financial burden, and also to get a diverse spread of experience and opinion. Paddy's first call was to Joe Linders, one of our partners in Belfield, who had a long history with Smithfield because his family car business was based there. Without hesitation, Joe signed up for a third of the deal.

The Bradys, who were our partners on a deal in Blackrock, were also cut in for 10 per cent. They had been trying to acquire the site from Charlie Duffy for a few years and we felt they should have a seat at the table. The Kellys and the Flynns split the remaining stake.

I called Aidan Marsh in Beauchamps solicitors to tell him what was needed. Aidan, a great property lawyer and also a great problem solver, had been the solicitor on most of our deals to date. We were going to have a lot of title issues in Smithfield because of the nature of the deeds, and he was just the right person to manage this complex process.

I gave him the details of Charlie's solicitor and added that we needed to complete the deal by the following day.

'We can't do it in one day,' Aidan said.

'We have to, that's the deal, and we're worried about Liam,' I told him. Liam Carroll had been sniffing around the site for a while, but Charlie was tired of waiting for him to meet his price. 'The CPO is going to clean up any title problems, so get it done,' was my message to Aidan.

'There's lots of risk here,' Aidan said, referring to the title and its quirks.

'You're well able to sort it out,' I assured him, and we left it at that. He knew what we needed to achieve and we trusted him to get us there. We wanted lawyers who could get things done, rather than lawyers who told us not to do it. Yes-men were busy, and maybe-men got nowhere in this market.

With the legal element under way, we just had the simple matter of the money to worry about. On a deal structured like this, the bank would not be able to take a charge on the site, which always made them nervous. They had to find a way to lend us the first million so that it didn't look like a total flyer. The loan would be based on our ability to get the deal done and deliver a viable project.

We had our loan offer from Anglo later that day and it was on the usual terms: a 3 per cent margin on the money and a 1 per cent fee. The initial €1 million was only the small end of the financing requirement. The real negotiation would come when we got to the closing of the site and paying over the balance of €7 million. The construction facility, which would be at least €150 million, would be on top of this.

All through that first day of the deal, I didn't believe we would get over the line within twenty-four hours. It was a crazy deadline, but by some miracle we made it. Within a day of shaking hands on a deal, we had contracted to buy one of the largest available sites in the city centre, in a great location, for only €1 million down. It was a classic Paddy deal. Now we had to make it work.

We called up the Belfield Office Park professional team, led by HKR Architects, and immediately started thinking about planning permission. We had to use the two-year payment window to add real value to the site if we were to be confident of finding the €7 million to close the deal.

That was the part of the project that Paddy loved. Planning permission is his thing: he has a great ability to get the maximum from a site, bringing everybody along with him. Jerry Ryan, our architect from HKR, and he immediately set about planning the scheme and identifying Smithfield's relevance to Dublin. We quickly prepared a vision document on the square and comparable urban spaces around the world. There was still a monthly horse fair in the square, which brought great colour though not a lot of commercial activity to other businesses in the vicinity. The market traders had already left the area, so it was generally quiet apart from the Children's Court. The city council had been looking to give the square a new civic prominence and they had recently used it as a music venue and a finishing point for the Dublin Marathon — which I'd run for the fifth time that year.

The locals had not been so happy with the new agenda for the square and took a particular dislike to the concerts. A challenge that we were going to have in this development was to align the interests of the city council, the interests of the locals, and our need to make a profit.

We had to get a lot of buildings on to our site to maximize the profits, and argued that the square could take tall buildings around it because of the scale of the open space. Over the next few months, the plans were prepared in conjunction with the city council and the scheme began to take shape. Initially we were looking for a large amount of office space in it. The council wanted a higher residential proportion, to bring life to the area at night. We agreed on a mix, with apartments facing on to the square and offices at the back. The council also asked us to include a hotel and we put in a simple three-star.

We had yet to acquire the full site, and while we worked away on the plan Joe Linders was busy buying up the bits we did not own. They were a mix of small sites, old leases and unknown bits of title. Our line was the same with every owner: 'If you don't sell to us, the council will CPO your land.'

Initially people had put up a fight, but we were the only game in town and the CPO was too big a threat when compared with a reasonable commercial offer from us.

We got stuck on two parts of the site, which took some special attention. The first was a small plot owned by Liam Carroll. He had bought it with a view to owning the entire site and we assumed his ambitions were very close to ours. Now he was trying to use his part as a ransom strip. If the CPO had not been hanging over it, it would have been a real problem for us: without a CPO, the only way to obtain the entire site we wanted would have been to pay Liam's ransom. We needed the council to help with his part of the site because they dealt with Liam a lot more than we did. He had a legendary relationship with the council that he had built up over the years. He had acquired his apartment empire in large part by buying land from the council at knockdown prices. Eventually the council managed to convince him to move aside. We never found out the details of the deal they had to do.

The final piece of the jigsaw was a portion of the north end of the site owned by the Wickhams, an old fruit-trading family. When I got the message in Druids Glen about the planning, I made a call to get the details. That was when I learned that we had got our planning but the Wickhams had failed in theirs. Their planning permission had a similar mix to ours and they seemed to have failed based on the design of their buildings. This was the opportunity we needed, and we quickly stepped in to buy their part of the site. We now owned and controlled the full 4.25 acres.

There is nothing quite as painful for a property developer as waiting for objections after planning permission has been granted, then dealing with them. We had two in Smithfield. One was from the local community organization, Macro. It can be very tricky and very expensive dealing with community organizations. The other was from An Taisce. Their objection was specific to a building at the north end of the site, which faced some Georgian buildings. Normally nobody can deal with An Taisce, and a trip to An Bord Pleanála didn't suit our timeline.

We quickly came to a deal with Macro to provide them with some free property and funding for local activities. They seemed to want the area to be developed, and this gave us great leverage with An Taisce. With the locals and the corporation firmly behind our plans, we strongly encouraged An Taisce to roll in with us. After a few meetings, agreement was reached and we changed a few small design details to address their fears about the density of the project.

The development specified in our planning permission was very dense and the average height of our buildings was eight storeys. The city council had granted us a twenty-three-storey tower in the middle of our scheme, and that was the only real victim of the planning objections.

While we had been working on the deal and the planning permission, the world had gone through a series of major economic shocks: the dotcom crash, a US recession, and the 11 September attacks. The Irish property market was deemed too hot by the government and they had implemented some of the recommendations on the Bacon Report to restrict investor buying. Tax breaks, which were a feature of Smithfield, had been cut back somewhat, and new rules had been brought in, requiring the inclusion of social and affordable housing in new developments. Individually neither of those was very significant, but put together they had a very negative effect on the numbers.

The government had been surprised by the negative reaction to their Bacon measures and we were happy to hear them reversed on Budget Day in 2002 by Charlie McCreevy. I was even happier the next day when I got a call from Kieran Ryan, our tax adviser and accountant.

'I have good news for you,' Kieran said.

'I saw the budget, so I know,' was my answer.

'I have even better news,' he said.

'What?' I asked, wondering what he could mean.

'Hidden in the detail of the budget, they have given you full capital allowances for Smithfield,' Kieran said. I could visualize the smile on his face.

The Bacon measures had restricted the capital allowances available to urban-renewal developments. In the small print of the budget, however, the minister for finance had just restored full capital allowances in Smithfield and other designated sites, provided we started building immediately. Those allowances would enable us to add 20 per cent to our apartment prices, and that in turn jacked up the land value. The industry had lobbied hard against the anti-investor parts of the Bacon measures and this was a pivotal win we had not expected.

It was great news for the project, and it influenced how we would build out the scheme. Initially we had looked at constructing the development in three separate phases. It was common to phase a development of this scale because building it all at once was a huge challenge, both physically and financially. Charlie McCreevy had given us the incentive to start immediately and the obligation to work fast if we were to keep the maximum capital allowances.

A few months after that announcement, I met the minister at the launch of a new stockbroking company in the Shelbourne Hotel. After his speech, I approached him and thanked him for the removal of the Bacon measures. I told him they had been a real dampener on the market, and that Smithfield would now progress immediately, thanks to his budget. His response to this was that he never liked to intervene in the market, and that the Bacon measures were an intervention and therefore wrong. As I turned away to talk to somebody else, a thought entered my head: Does he not see that tax breaks are a huge intervention on the market? I wondered for days after that conversation if the government really understood the power of capital allowances. I certainly did, having witnessed their effects in Tallaght and now Smithfield. It was not for us to write the rules, merely to play by the ones we were handed.

After the amazing news on the tax allowances we quickly mobilized the project. We had to move fast and cut a few corners where possible. The buildings were a long way from being fully designed, so the only way that we could work out a construction budget was to start with a bill of rates and fill in the quantities as we went along. That made the bank very nervous, because in theory construction costs could spiral out of control. Anglo had been very worried about construction costs after a bad experience with the development of the Four Seasons Hotel in Ballsbridge. Anglo was part of a club syndicate, led by ACC Bank, which was banking the development of the hotel. The developers had contracted to sell the hotel to a Quinlan-McCormack partnership for about £60 million. In theory the developer was to make a handsome profit on the deal, but the construction budget was wrong and it turned out that the hotel was going to cost more than £60 million to build. The problem for Anglo was that they didn't find this out until about £60 million had been spent. The banks had to step in to the deal and complete the hotel, taking a loss of more than £10 million in the process. They were forced to do this because a contract bound the development companies to deliver the hotel fully completed. If the banks had not stepped in, the hotel would have been forced to sit incomplete and in litigation, which would have greatly increased their loss. Anglo hated to take a loss on any loan, so they were now paranoid about construction costs all over town. In the past we had always been left to worry about construction costs: I do not remember any bank really questioning me on my numbers on either the cost side or the value side. Now Anglo wanted Bruce Shaw, their favoured quantity surveyors, to sign off on every project, looking over our shoulder along the way, and we had to pay a fee for this. It felt like a waste but it was now a fact of life. I called it 'Four Seasons Flu'.

Not many firms in Ireland could handle a project of the size of our Smithfield development. Pierse were our partners and contractors on the IFSC developments, so we had to let them have a shot, and Cramptons built Belfield Office Park for us, so they were also on the list. A few other builders tried to get involved through their various contacts, but we limited the tender to these two and told them it was a two-horse race so that they came forward with their best numbers. We were looking for the best builder to deliver the project at a reasonable price, and we felt that limiting the tender field would bring out a fair one.

Tony Cooney, our quantity surveyor on the deal, worked only for developers, never for builders, so he was never trying to keep a contractor happy at our expense. The bank's quantity surveyors are generally from a much larger firm, and act for everybody, so I am never certain about their conflicts of interest. Tony's allegiance was not in question, and he was a central part of our cost management team. I liked the way he operated: when you got a number from him, you knew it would be right at the end of the project. There would be no Four Seasons Flu with Tony on the job. He also knew us well, and he built room into his budgets to allow us a little bit of quality. We wanted to leave our mark on Smithfield, and we would not be cutting the construction budget too fine. The tax breaks gave us space to do a great job.

Smithfield was an enormous construction project and, from an engineering point of view, we would use many groundbreaking technologies that had not been tried in Dublin before. The basement was three storeys deep – the largest and deepest basement ever built in Dublin – and we were going to dig it out in one phase. That alone would take at least a year to build, and at the end of the project there would be more than twelve acres of car parking for over a thousand cars. The main challenge in constructing a basement is keeping it dry and stopping it floating. A basement as large as Smithfield's, and three storeys deep, is more like a ship than a building: if we moved it down to the port, it would float away and it would be larger than most ships. The weight of the building we constructed over the basement would counteract the basement's natural buoyancy, but even with all the steel and concrete overhead, huge ground anchors would be needed to stop the buildings floating away.

While the basement got under way, I began to work out how much money we would need. Anglo had provided us with an initial facility to get started and avail ourselves of the tax allowances. It was up to Kieran Duggan and me to work out the details on the big facility to build out the whole scheme. The standard 3 per cent margin that we paid for all Anglo development money was never part of the negotiations: it was a given. We had heard rumours from other developers of the bank doing deals at 2 per cent, but we were pretty happy with our rate: we knew that in exchange we would get the flexibility we needed.

The main point of contention was the fee.

'We're happy at the usual one per cent,' I told Kieran.

'You must be joking, Simon,' Kieran replied. 'Nobody else would fund this.'

That may or may not have been true, but finding funding elsewhere was not a challenge I relished. 'I know that, but one per cent will be two million euro. It's a big number,' I argued.

'Two hundred million is a big loan, Simon, and we need two per cent,' Kieran said.

Smithfield was the biggest development project in the city, with the exception of Spencer Dock. The change in the tax allowances had forced us to move away from our three-phase plan: to receive the tax breaks that were vital to the scheme, we had to start immediately and get completed within three years. That meant we needed Anglo's €200 million.

I like Kieran so I was a little soft on him with the fee. (Also, as an Anglo shareholder, I was glad to see the bank firming up on their charges. I figured that I could hedge the extra cost of their fee by buying more shares in the bank. During the negotiations on the Smithfield debt, Steve and I bought more through CFDs with IG Index. The margin on the shares had now been reduced to 10 per cent and this allowed us lots of leverage. We had noticed the volumes in the stock rising steeply, and Anglo was now a regular feature on the investor chat boards. International money had arrived on the Anglo share register.)

Kieran and I finally settled on a fee of 1.625 per cent. He agreed to this compromise with one condition: if we needed more than the €200 million (and he thought we would), the fee would go up to the full 2 per cent. In total I had calculated that the bank would receive fees and interest of about €22 million on the deal and that their profit would be about €15 million.

I called a meeting of our partners to run through the final terms. We arranged to meet at our offices at 128 Baggot Street. This was the biggest deal that any of us had ever done and the most money we had ever borrowed. As usual with an Anglo loan, we would all be on the line personally for the money, so we needed to make sure we were happy to go forward.

'The fee is huge,' one partner said.

'It's too generous for the bank,' another jumped in.

I explained that 1.625 per cent was the lowest Anglo would go, and that they were the only bank who would finance us. Our target profit for the project was €60 million after paying the bank their fees and interest, and we had no equity in the deal, which was a huge added bonus. 'It's being one hundred per cent financed by Anglo so we should not begrudge the bank a little profit,' I told the meeting, trying to get them to see sense. I couldn't believe they thought that the bank was overcharging for the money. We were getting to build out a risky property development with 100 per cent bank money, and the only real cost was standard interest plus a bonus fee. I thought the bank should be getting a profit share, for the risk they were taking, but I didn't say so to anybody.

'If you think the fee is too high, just buy their shares,' was my closing comment. I think I was the only shareholder in the room – most property developers hated the idea of buying shares, even bank shares: 'Why buy shares when you can buy land?' was the general developer view. Mine would have been the reverse. Shares you can sell when you need cash. Land is a little more difficult to get rid of.

After all the talking, we agreed to take the deal. There was no real alternative, but it was important to have the discussion as a group. We were about to sign up personally for €200 million of debt.

At the end of the meeting John Flynn threw in a curveball. 'I think Liam Carroll would buy the site from us now,' he said. 'What do you think?'

'That we should look at it,' I said.

None of us really wanted to sell because we were excited by the scale of the project. Still, we felt we'd better consider it. It can be reassuring to everyone involved to get an offer that would bring a large profit, even if the offer is not accepted. It boosts everybody's confidence, including that of the bank.

The Flynns were pretty close to CBRE, the international estate agents, who were very close to Liam Carroll. The word was put out that we were interested in an offer on the site. Up to that point, our total cost was about €30 million and we had the full site ready to develop. Only Liam would have the capacity and the desire to do that. After a few days, John got back to me on the phone. 'Sixty million is where he's at,' John said.

'That's too low,' I said. 'We can make more building it out.'

I had hoped that Liam would be closer to €80 million, and we might have sold him the site for that kind of money. I was excited about building the scheme out, but a big offer would help me deal with the disappointment of having to move on. Paddy, however, was dead set against selling the site to Liam Carroll at any price. He felt that the planning permission had been given to him as much as to the plan for the site. Selling it to Liam now would be a slap in the face to the city council because Liam would not build to the same specification and quality as we intended.

'We cannot be seen as speculators flipping land on,' Paddy said to me, in the office.

'I don't think they'd mind,' I said. 'They deal with Liam Carroll everywhere else.'

'I know, but Smithfield is special. They really want it to be great, and they won't want us to sell it,' Paddy said.

In the end, we didn't get the knockout offer we had hoped for from Liam Carroll and we settled down for a few years of construction and project management.

For all the scope and ambition of the Smithfield project, it was by no means my obsession at this time. I had been dealing on a number of fronts in the IFSC and the South Docks. The Clarion Hotel had been completed to acclaim, we had won more tenders in the IFSC, and we had been approached to construct more Clarions around the country.

We had successfully tendered for and won the right to develop apartments on a site adjoining the Clarion in the IFSC. The hotel had achieved such recognition that we were going to name the apartment development Clarion Quay. It was a profit-share deal with the DDDA based upon award-winning architecture. They had staged a competition for the design of the scheme and had then put this out to tender. We had lined up a great array of retail tenants, including the restaurant chain Milano, AIB and Marks & Spencer, and we intended to retain those shops as an investment while selling off the apartments. That had become our game plan all over town: hold on to the commercial rental income, and sell off the residential.

I had a good look at the possibility of holding on to the residential portion of the schemes that we developed. With the market rising so fast every year, it seemed a pity to leave profit behind. The issue for me with apartments was that managing them was a big hassle. Commercial tenants leave you alone unless there is a major issue, whereas residential tenants never do.

Demand for apartments across Dublin had never been stronger and we were selling out schemes on the launch day almost every time. Selling at least a hundred apartments in one day now seemed the norm. To be a developer in Dublin made for a very busy life in that kind of market, and we rarely stopped to celebrate our success. Selling €25 million worth of apartments at a launch hardly merited comment, and our main challenge in selling them was not to undercharge. We were always pushing the price up, but we needed to make sure that it was within the constraints of demand.

The biggest social extravagance I stretched to in those busy days was a rare snatched lunch in Diep Le Shaker with Brian and Alan McCormack. We tried to get together every few months to check where we were on various projects, and there was no better place to do this than at Diep over some hot food and cool wine.

The Anglo social offers came thick and fast, but they mostly involved golf and I passed on almost all of those events. They got me to the Wimbledon final once with my wife, but that was the limit of the bank-fuelled corporate entertainment I accepted. I had a niggling feeling that I was not maxing my entertainment credits with the bank, and that I could have been asking to go anywhere. Once in a while they would ask me what I liked, and I'd tell them that what I liked they couldn't give. I wanted to go home in the early afternoon and relax with my wife and children on a sunny day at our house in Wicklow, where we had moved.

'What about Barcelona for the Grand Prix?' they would suggest.

'No, thanks. I'll watch it on TV,' I'd reply.

'Ireland versus Italy in Rome?' they would tempt me.

'A day away from the phone,' was my request, but of course they couldn't grant that.

It did strike me as a little strange that I wanted to work
that hard, handling millions of euro, so I could stay at home
and spend no money. I seemed to be aiming for the moon,
when I really wanted to get down the road.

Deals seemed a bit like rabbits: once you saw one, you knew
there must be hundreds. They bred at a similar rate. One led
to two, two led to four, and four led to God knew where.
Deals were easy to start and hard to wrap up, and managing
the partnership relationship was a real challenge. Everybody
wanted to be part of the team, and sometimes I felt the team
had grown too large to manage.

Paddy saw the partnerships as our strength. We would partner with almost anybody and, in a rising market, all
partnerships seemed profitable, which tended to keep the
peace. I found the partnerships to be a weakness because we
were part of everything but in control of nothing. We didn't
control the bank, or the deal, and we always seemed to be
carrying our partners along. Where we drove, they followed,
but being at the front, driving all the time, began to wear me
out a little.

Slowly, I hatched a new plan.

5. Other People's Money

'I think I can rent upstairs to Boundary Capital,' David Kelly said to me, over coffee one morning in the summer of 2005. He worked on the finance and project-management end of our schemes. The top two floors of our office on Baggot Street had been empty for a few months, so getting them let would be good news. We wanted a friendly tenant and Boundary would be perfect.

I had approached David about joining our management team a number of years earlier, when he was chief financial officer at Chartbusters, the video rental chain, in which we had a 30 per cent ownership stake.

Over a long Chinese lunch in Stillorgan, I explained to David the nature of the property-development business. I told him we needed somebody to put manners on it and keep it under control. The numbers had got very big, yet our management team had hardly grown. It felt as though I was doing everything, and hiring David was my first step towards moving the business from a purely family affair to a corporate enterprise. David jumped at the chance, and I had my right-hand man.

With David came a host of connections in the business world. Through him, I heard about Niall McFadden and the dark world of corporate finance. Niall McFadden had risen through the ranks of the venture-capital community, and he quickly realized that he wanted to be the promoter of a corporate-finance business rather than an employee. He had done a number of big deals in Dublin, starting with the take-private of Riverdeep, soon followed by the takeover of Arnotts plc. In buying Arnotts, Niall had set up an investment company called Boundary Capital, which would be our new neighbour and tenant upstairs in 128 Lower Baggot Street.

'With Niall upstairs, we might get some business together,' I told David. No doubt David had also seen this angle. Corporate finance mixed with property might be very productive.

Over the first few months we were all busy and all kept to ourselves, with only the odd encounter in the reception area or the hall. Boundary were busy on their corporate-finance work and we were busy on our property work. There was little to indicate, from these early months, the force that was about to be unleashed.

Up to that point in the property business, we had acted in partnership with a number of developers buying land and constructing buildings. This process was certainly working from a financial point of view, but there were always tensions in the relationships. Developers have large egos, which make for regular clashes. I was also getting tired of dealing with Anglo. The money was becoming harder to extract and the bank was getting harder to deal with because of the scale of the business and the numbers involved. The loans kept being approved, but the detail and the paperwork were becoming more complex. Kieran Duggan had moved on, and I didn't have the energy to deal with new bankers all the time. They were nice people, but the magic of breakfast in the Shelbourne had passed. The bank now wanted to look at the deal, rather than back the man. Anglo was becoming more like AIB or Bank of Ireland, even as the big old banks were becoming more like old Anglo.

I knew there was a better way because I had seen it in Tallaght all those years ago. Derek Quinlan had it all, from my point of view. He could do any deal he wanted because he had the firepower of OPM: other people's money. We had often taken OPM into deals in the past, bringing partners into our deals, but the problem with that kind of money was that it wanted to know about the deal and get involved in the detail. Not everybody can have their opinion valued in a hundred-million-euro development scheme. People are excluded from the decision-making process because decisions need to be made now, and now does not allow for a long discussion. That is where the tension arises. I wanted the new OPM model to have a different angle, and seeing how Niall operated gave me this angle. Corporate finance does not do opinion or debate. The investor writes a cheque, backing the management team, and after a few years he gets his money out, plus a nice profit and less the appropriate fee. Peering into that world, I quickly became envious of the nature of their OPM. It didn't talk at all. It was just money, with no personality or baggage. The money seemed to beg to get into some of the deals, but once it was in, it had to keep quiet and stay in the background.

As I began to look at their model, I was quickly attracted to the fee structure: '2 and 20', as it is called in the hedge-fund business. The promoter gets 2 per cent of the capital value of a project as an annual management fee, and on top of this he also gets 20 per cent of the profits.

David brokered the channel between Niall and me on a potential link-up to raise some equity for a deal. Almost every site that came on the market in Dublin was being offered to us for sale, and linking up this deal flow with Niall's ability to raise equity and finance was attractive.

In late 2005 I was looking at an interesting deal in Dun Laoghaire where a vacant 1980s office building was being offered to me. Nobody seemed very interested in bidding for it, myself included. The building was occupied by a tenant, but they were breaking the lease early and paying six years' rent to get out. That seemed crazy to me, but it was an institutional tenant, and there's no accounting for their logic. The ESB pension fund was selling the building, and the six years' rent was being discounted off the price. Basically the pension fund wanted to sell because the building was going to become vacant, and the tenant urgently wanted out. They both needed to sell as quickly as possible to get what they wanted. In the end I agreed to buy the building for €6 million, with a long closing date. The tenants topped up my payment by almost €5 million. For €6 million, I had bought a building that was valued by the pension fund at €11 million. Obviously there was no rental income, but that was where I hoped to make my money.

I got on the phone and made the usual call to Anglo to arrange the deposit cheque. After I had explained the bargain I was getting, Anglo sent over the cheque.

David suggested that the Dun Laoghaire building could be our first deal with Niall McFadden. I arranged a lunch with Niall and Paddy. We booked a table at L'Écrivain to go through the details. Paddy had hardly been involved in this first small deal but I certainly wanted to get him fully involved in the future of the venture. I thought: This is the vehicle and the model that can finally liberate us to be pure developers, without the burden and bother of finance.

Niall and I walked up to the restaurant together and were led to our table. There was a gang from Anglo having a party in the private dining room, which was near the front door. I waved at them through the glass partition and walked up the stairs with Niall to the main dining room on the first floor. The restaurant was packed but the noise level was low. There was plenty of room between the tables, and this was the perfect place to discuss and celebrate a deal. We took our table by the window, and Niall ordered a bottle of white wine. Today would be one of those rare days when we drank at lunch, because we both knew that something big might come out of the deal.

'Is Paddy with you on this?' Niall asked me.

'Yes. I've explained the whole thing to him,' I replied.

'What about your partners? Will they mind?' Niall said.

'I expect so, but that's their problem,' I said.

Niall was a little worried that our new partnership would cause a split in our old ones. People had become used to us buying land on their behalf and this new move would clearly be seen as an end to that. We would be on our own.

'We have enough deals with them all to last a lifetime,' I told Niall.

'I know that, and I want to buy a few of those deals off you,' he replied.

Niall can smell money like a shark can smell blood, and he certainly smelt it here. He saw no limit to the amount of equity that could be raised for the property business, and in us he saw the deals that could absorb all that money. I was excited about being able to do deals without the finance workload, and I was also interested in selling a few sites to the new company. In fact, I would have been happy to see most of our portfolio pass over in some kind of sale, but I held this to myself – it was too much for that meeting.

Paddy arrived and sat down to join us. Niall dressed like a finance guy, while Paddy and I looked like relaxed developers. People in the room recognized Paddy, and probably Niall, and the whispers began.

'What shall we call it?' was Paddy's opening remark.

Niall was slightly taken aback by that because he presumed that we still had to convince Paddy that it was a good model to adopt. In fact, I had already sold Paddy on the plan so no convincing was needed. We agreed that OPM was the way forward.

'You decide,' was Niall's answer, deferring to the more experienced man.

'You're Boundary and we're Redquartz. Maybe we should call it Boundary Redquartz,' Paddy replied.

'It's a big clunky,' said Niall. 'What about Redquartz Boundary, or RQB for short?' That settled it. RQB had a nice ring.

Our business would be the acquisition of sites and development assets, using OPM and charging fees and a carry. The carry would be in the form of a profit share for us as promoters. We would earn 20 per cent of the profits on every deal once the investor had received their base return of 10 per cent. This was a typical hedge-fund structure and it allowed the promoters to earn large amounts of profit using OPM. Paddy and I would find the opportunities and Boundary would structure the finance. We were all certain that this would grow big.

Niall had one condition on the deal. 'I need you both to focus fully on RQB, and I want every new deal to be an RQB deal,' he said.

'That's fine by us,' I replied. 'We want to be fully committed to this business.'

Niall was forceful on this issue because he wanted the business to be above reproach. All Kelly deals would be offered to RQB, which meant we could never be accused of double-dealing. That level of scrutiny had not always been in place with other Irish property companies. With every deal being on offer to RQB, we could not be accused of holding certain deals aside for ourselves. Our total commitment to RQB was genuine: I believed that it was the best model for the property-development business. I longed for the end of the personality developer with the Anglo cheque book, and the emergence of properly capitalized property companies.

Niall's team took on the full finance and equity role on the initial deal. We stuck with Anglo, because they wrote the deposit cheque, but we firmed up on the terms and got the debt with a very limited personal guarantee. That was the first loan I ever did with Anglo where I did not sign the standard personal guarantee.

I'm beginning to like this, I thought.

Doing a deal and buying a building creates great excitement and satisfaction, and that was the main buzz in the property business. To get that feeling without the hassle of chasing the money or dealing with the bank was brilliant. It was like having all gain without the pain.

The first deal didn't follow the true OPM model: 75 per cent of the funding came from Anglo, and the 25 per cent equity came from a small group connected to Niall and ourselves. Once we had the first success in place, we hoped to hit the street and raise some real equity for bigger deals.

The plan for the Dun Laoghaire building was very much a hit-and-run. It was an out-of-date 1980s office building and there was not too much demand for that type of space in Dun Laoghaire. My plan was to convert the ground floor to retail use, and the top three floors to apartments. That would leave only two floors of offices, which I had broken up into small units for accountants or solicitors to buy. The building would get a new front and a modernized interior, but the work would be very limited. I thought we could sell the building on to a developer or builder once we'd got the planning permission in place. It was a classic developer plan: take an unpolished gem from an institutional investor and apply some style and creativity to make a profit.

We hit our normal stride on the planning permission, using a recently departed team from HKR Architects to do the work. They gave us a great plan for a keen fee, and the planners in Dun Laoghaire loved the idea of tidying up those old office blocks, getting retail into the ground floor and life on to the street.

Within a few months of buying the building, we were looking good on the planning and the value had risen considerably. All we needed now was a buyer. We would start the process of finding one immediately the permission was fully granted.

We went about forming the new company, called RQB Ltd, as a fifty-fifty joint venture between Redquartz and Boundary. David Kelly and Alan Murphy would support Paddy and me as part of the Redquartz team, and Declan Cassidy – a long-time lieutenant of Niall's with a keen eye for detail – would step in with Niall.

This would be different from the normal staff-light developer model, because we intended to hire professional staff to fill every role. Paddy and I were on the board with Declan Cassidy, and Niall sat at the top as chairman. At our first meeting following the lunch, Niall said he thought we needed a new CEO to drive the business forward.

This was a new style to me, but I liked it. With Redquartz I had normally filled the role of CEO, being responsible for everything, and the idea of having a real CEO sounded great. 'Any idea who?' I asked Niall.

'I've been working on a guy in Anglo who I think would be good,' Niall said.

'Can you say who?' I asked.

'Paul Pardy,' Niall answered, and I think he saw my stunned look.

Paul Pardy was one of the top lenders in Anglo, and I'd

assumed he would be staying there for a long time. I had had extensive dealings with him when he was under the wing of Kieran Duggan. The connection slowly began to click in my mind: I remembered Paul speaking very highly of Niall at a meeting a number of years ago. Back then, he'd told me I must meet Niall McFadden and that we would get along very well.

Immediately after the meeting, I dialled Paul's number on my BlackBerry and he answered on the first ring. We both broke out laughing.

'Strange world,' I told him.

'Very strange,' Paul answered.

'We should meet up and have a coffee. Are you around tomorrow?' I asked.

'Name the place. Somewhere different,' Paul offered.

'Not the Shelbourne, then. Let's try the Morrison at eleven.'

I was getting the feeling that this could run and run. McFadden, Kelly and Pardy: Dublin had never seen anything like it. The buzz was back. This beat building another hundred apartments: for the first time I felt as though I was really building a business. To that point the business had seemed like a series of one-night stands on individual deals; this felt like the real thing.

I was late to the Morrison, and when I arrived Paul was waiting for me in the lobby, sitting over his second coffee and looking a little nervous. Normally when I met him, I was the one needing approval, hoping to get the money. This time it was different. I could tell from the moment the meeting started that he was dying to get out of Anglo and longed to sit on my side of the table.

'Are you ready for the dark side?' I asked him. Anglo had spat out a number of senior guys in the past and some had struggled in the real world. In Anglo, you didn't need to call anybody because they called you. On the outside, you had to make it happen.

'I'm ready,' Paul said, and I knew he meant it.

Paul wore his heart on his sleeve and it was clear that it was going to happen. We talked about his wife and family and the support he had at home for the move. We wrapped up the meeting knowing we were going into business together. I left Niall to tidy up the contract and the terms. Paul would be earning more with RQB than he had ever made with Anglo. He was a developer now and would be getting developer money. A key part of the deal for Paul was that he would own 15 per cent of the business. At Anglo, he was an employee and maybe a small shareholder, but in RQB he would be a partner. We had to make a couple of calls to Anglo to smooth the way for Paul – and we certainly didn't want to upset them by being seen to poach their staff. The bank were broad-minded about the move and they wished Paul the best of luck.

With Paul in place, we upped the pace again. I had had two site-purchase deals go through the Anglo credit committee in previous weeks and Paul had noticed them. One was for a site at Blackpitts, off Clanbrassil Street just west of Dublin city centre, which I had agreed to buy for €12.2 million, and the other was €17 million for land in Kilkenny.

'I've got to get the Blackpitts deal,' Paul said, with hunger in his eyes.

Blackpitts was a deal I had tried my best not to buy, so selling it on to RQB at a profit was not a great burden. My chance to buy the land in Blackpitts came about because I had bought a pub on the corner of the site a few years previously. I'd made this initial purchase at the behest of my uncle, and the deal was funded by Bank of Scotland – an indicator of my lack of ambition for the site. I'd thought it would be a slow-burning deal so I kept it away from Anglo; and it worked to do it with Bank of Scotland because they were looking to be more aggressive with their development lending. My uncle knew the adjoining owners, who ran a scrap-metal business, so he was more optimistic. Over the two years since we had bought the pub, we had courted the scrap merchants for a deal. They played the usual cagey game, and our approaches came to nothing. We settled in to run the pub, and let some time pass.

When I saw the tender board go up on the adjoining site I thought it would be a good chance to sell the pub to whoever bought the site. The pub cost €1.5 million and I might get a nice turn if a keen developer bought the land. DTZ were trying to drum up interest in the site, but I ignored their overtures. RQB had not yet gained traction and I needed a new site in Dublin like a hole in the head.

With a few days left before the tender date, Peter Lynch in DTZ began to ring me with an edge in his voice. 'Come on, Simon, make a bid,' he pleaded.

'No, thanks,' I told him. 'Make sure you tell the buyer that I'll sell the pub for two point five million euro.' I liked the idea of moving on and making a quick million, and I hoped that being clear about my price might encourage somebody to buy from me early. The pub was a kind of ransom strip, but I was clear with Peter that I would sell for €2.5 million, which was far from a ransom price.

On the day of the tender I ignored the deadline of twelve o'clock and went about my business with other meetings. I hoped to get a call from Peter at some stage looking to buy the pub. Whoever wanted to develop the site would need to own it so I knew I would make a profit at some point. About three o'clock I saw Peter's number flash up on the BlackBerry.

'How did it go?' I asked him.

'You didn't bid,' he said.

'Of course not. I told you I wouldn't.'

'Will you bid now?'

'Oh, no, Peter – you got no bids,' I said, with genuine regret. 'I don't want it.'

'Simon, I need you here. It's a great site. Please, please, please.'

'It's Christmas, Peter. Let's wait till January,' I said, trying to get off the phone.

'They're worried about tomorrow's Budget and they need a deal,' Peter said, and that gave it all away: the scrap dealers were desperate to get a deal to secure the 20 per cent tax rate. Rumours were flying around town about a change in the tax structure, and landowners like the scrap dealers were getting very nervous.

The guide price on the land was €15 million.

'I'll pay ten million euro,' I told Peter, trying to get rid of him, but beginning to play on his desperation.

'That's too low, but I'll come back to you,' he said, to my amazement.

A few minutes later, my phone rang again. I was walking around a factory in west Dublin, looking at shop fittings, and it was not a great place or time to negotiate a land deal.

'Twelve million,' he said.

'OK, but I am not busting my arse to get a contract in place,' I replied.

'We have to have a contract,' Peter said, and I knew that this was the case, because the scrap dealers needed to cover off the tax risk.

'I'll pay a hundred K deposit next week, and let's sign the contract tomorrow. I'll need a long closing as well,' I offered.

'A hundred K? Come on, Simon. It's twelve million,' Peter pleaded.

'A hundred K or leave. Tell them the Budget is tomorrow.'

That's how the site was bought. Despite my best efforts, I had bought the land. We had certainly got a great deal – and now we had the site with which Paul wanted to launch RQB.

If the deal in Dun Laoghaire was like a small starter for RQB, then the site in Blackpitts was going to be a nice juicy steak: a real development deal with all the frills. I had got Peter to agree to a long closing for the site and I used the time to get the planning permission agreed and lodged with Dublin City Council. That meant that by the time we were raising the equity for the deal through RQB, the good-news flow would have started, and the value of the site would start to rise.

The development I planned was a mixed scheme of about 150 apartments, some retail units and an office building of about 35,000 square feet. I would have preferred to build only apartments, a sure thing in the location, but we had to include the offices and retail because the land was zoned for a mix of residential and commercial use. We hired Hamilton Osborne King (HOK) to review the apartment plans and their potential pricing, and even I was surprised by how bullish they were. They were pricing the apartments as if they were on St Stephen's Green.

I was getting congratulations from all corners as if this was the deal of the century, and all I kept thinking about was how I had tried not to buy it.

'The office and the retail are going to be a problem,' I told Paul.

'We'll pre-sell them so don't worry,' he said. That was an old trick we all used. There was excitement and fervour at the launch stage of a project, which could never be re-created at the end when reality was delivered. This was especially true in urban-renewal projects like Blackpitts, where the adjoining sites were very run down.

'We need to use this project to attract as many clients as possible,' Paul suggested.

'I think the equity is about five million euro,' I said.

'Let's raise more. Let's get eight million and build up clients,' Paul said.

'And let's limit each investor to a hundred K,' Niall added.

'Why?' I asked.

'To build clients. We'll get eighty clients on this deal, and they'll all make money,' Niall answered.

Nothing spreads faster than the rumour of a good deal and fast profits. If we pulled this off, we would have eighty people extolling the virtues of RQB and money would never be a problem again. We wrapped up the meeting and jumped on to our phones as we walked out of the room. We were on our way.

Paul hit the street with the equity team and began to round up the cash. His contact book was bulging from his time in Anglo, and a lot of these contacts owed him a favour from his time there. Now he started to draw down this credit, getting clients to back him in his new adventure with RQB. The money was raised in a number of weeks. I sold on the pub to the syndicate for a profit of €1 million and went looking for more opportunities.

If I needed any further encouragement, I got it at the legal completion for the Blackpitts deal. The day a deal legally closes usually involves a scramble for cash as unforeseen problems arise. I always ended up at the closing writing a personal cheque to pay some legal fee or stamp duty. It was never great news for my bank manager when the cheque hit the account a few days later.

'It's for a closing,' I'd tell him, when he called. 'It'll come back in a few days.'

'You can't keep writing cheques that push you over your

limit,' he would answer, clearly stressed from trying to manage my account. 'Come in and we'll arrange an overdraft.'

'I don't want an overdraft. I just want to be able to write a cheque if I really need to,' I answered. I knew only too well that I would abuse an overdraft and constantly live at its limit if I was given one. It was better to have the limit at zero, and work from there.

I always used bank accounts as though there was no limit anyway, and the banks pretty much let me get away with this. I would get a hammering on the phone, but the money would be cleared. I would promise to get a lodgment to them the next day, and then the scramble would begin.

For the Blackpitts closing we had raised the €8 million from equity investors and there was another €8 million from the bank. That made it a very comfortable closing, and we had surplus cash at the end. For the first time in my life, I left the closing not having written any cheque and clutching my profit cheque of €1 million, plus a cheque for fees. That was like being paid to spend money. The best way for me to get more of this was to find more deals. The deals were a pain but the fees were great.

Scouting for land was my only official role at RQB, which suited me fine. When people know you have money, the land search is very easy. The offers just keep rolling in. But with very few exceptions, all the deals on offer were complete junk and I was not slow in telling people so. Everybody claimed to have the last great site in Dublin, and that made me laugh.

'I saw the last great site last week,' I would answer, when they talked up their deal. Everything was certainly for sale and everybody wanted a developer to be the buyer. It seemed that only the development angle could justify the premium that people were seeking.

Nearly every deal I didn't buy was snapped up by somebody

else, and this struck me as strange. Those deals were obviously junk, but somebody wanted the junk. To play in this market, we had to find the angles and skirt about the edges. That was how the next two deals came about.

We had run the rule over a house for sale in Foxrock, which was really a development site: every house in Foxrock with a large garden was now trading like a site. I have never really understood the Foxrock market. Everything always seemed too expensive to me, and the atmosphere of the place never struck a chord with me. Perfection is not an attractive characteristic, and Foxrock seemed to be full of houses and people seeking perfection. It was as if somebody had placed every tree for the maximum effect, and that created an overall air of artificiality.

We were going to the auction to try to build more perfect homes for plastic people. I had decided to stop trying to understand it and start trying to profit from it. The grass we were bidding on was getting Paul very excited, and he was pushing the value up.

He reckoned we should bid up to €30 million. I thought that was too high, but we had given Paul our backing so I didn't want to be too negative. As always, we broke our agreed limit and went well past €30 million, but somebody else was more spellbound than us by the site and paid over €40 million. That was a new high for land like that and it drove the overall market higher.

When a type of land is valued that highly, the logical thing to do is to look for a similar deal, and that was what we did. Paul knew of an opportunity near his home turf of Castleknock that was not selling because of services issues. When potential development land does not have access to sewers and connections, the value suffers considerably. As far as the market was concerned, this was the problem with the land at Diswellstown. The site was a grand Georgian house on 16.3 acres of development land, but the connection to the sewers was through land that belonged to Park Developments. There was no reliable map of sewers in Dublin and nobody seemed to know the routes of all the pipes. Paul got busy looking around the Diswellstown land and quietly found a sewer connection that was available to the site, without going through the Park Developments land. With this knowledge, we went ahead and agreed a deal on the land at €26 million. The angle had given us the competitive advantage, and we were the only bidder. The sellers still did well but the worries about the services had certainly taken €10 million off the value of the site. Paul's midnight search around the sewers of Dublin had proved fruitful.

That was deal three for RQB. We quickly raised the equity and got busy on the planning permission. People loved investing in Castleknock, and we took this on board for future deals. Location, location, location.

Deals four and five swiftly followed, with the acquisition of development land on the Naas Road and at Malahide. We raised the equity and bank debt with ease for all of those projects. The money just kept rolling in.

With a lot of buying under our belt we needed to turn some of the paper profits into real profits. We had just agreed to our first overseas mega-deal: $220 million for the Marriott Hotel and Resort at the Sawgrass Golf Club in Jacksonville, Florida. The deal was called 'Sawgrass' and this suited everybody, because we all wanted to imagine we were buying the actual golf course. Buying the Marriott didn't sound as good. The deal was the ultimate golf status game gone mad. All the years of playing golf had softened people's brains, in my view, and they had all convinced themselves that you needed to own a golf course to have any credibility. Owning a part of

Sawgrass was like owning a part of golf, and it got people really excited.

We needed to raise $90 million of equity and, despite the Sawgrass mystique, that seemed a lot for a company like RQB, which was still less than one year old.

'Let's sell some sites to help raise the money,' I said, at one of our regular meetings. We had planned to build out the sites, and the idea of selling early caused a stir. Paddy wasn't keen because he didn't want to be seen by Dublin City Council to be flipping sites. That was the Smithfield story playing over again. Niall, however, thought this was a great idea. The Blackpitts site seemed the best immediate candidate.

'Selling now will boost the IRR,' he noted. The internal rate of return on an investment was the only metric that corporate finance people respected. We targeted about 20 per cent for IRR, which meant that an investment would double in value every four years. Selling a deal early for a smaller profit could produce an IRR of more than 30 per cent, and our profit share in RQB was based on this, and not the overall return.

'We've got the planning, so let's just tender it and hopefully some dumb builder will take the bait,' I said. The buyers for those ready-to-go sites were generally builders looking to keep their team busy, or buying turnover. You could usually get one to bid you all the profit on a site with full planning permission. It never made sense to build out the developments when the builders were in that mood.

'HOK think it will fly,' I added. I had already had a chat with Stephen Cassidy of HOK about potentially selling the site, so they were lined up and ready.

'Let's do it,' Niall agreed. 'Once the investors get the profit in their hands, we'll have no problem on Sawgrass.' He had called it right: eighty investors flush with Blackpitts profit were the best advert for RQB, and we were pretty confident that most or all of the Blackpitts money, plus the profit, would be reinvested in other RQB deals, including Sawgrass.

We also agreed to sell the Naas Road site. We had not even lodged a planning application on it, but a site close by had just sold for over €5 million per acre and we would gladly walk for anything near that price. That would net us a profit of over €20 million for a twelve-month investment. The site had cost us only €18 million, or €2 million per acre.

We lined up both tenders for late 2006 and spent plenty of money on the marketing campaign. With HOK on board for Blackpitts, we retained HT Meagher O'Reilly for the Naas Road site. HT's James Meagher is a veteran of the market and knows all the big players. He was very confident about the site and the likely level of demand from developers.

With the Sawgrass fundraising well under way, the tender day for the sites loomed. We were selling both deals within a few months of each other. The first deal on the block was Blackpitts, and I was more confident about that one because it was in the centre of Dublin. It also had full planning permission and was 'ready to go', as we say in the business, which tends to pull in the builders.

HOK pushed as hard as they could and, come the tender day, were confident about the number of offers we might receive.

'I think we'll get five or six,' Stephen said, when I asked about the demand. We needed competition to get a good price, and five or six would be a great number. We were hoping to achieve a price of around €30 million for the site, which would be a nice profit on the original €15 million investment.

The tenders were normally sent to the solicitor for the seller, and that was how we set up this deal. In all my years in the property business, I had never been at a tender opening because we had never sold development land that way. I had always been the buyer. I was keen to attend the tender opening, but I couldn't make it and Paul was left alone with the solicitor.

After the appointed hour, which was twelve o'clock, I gave Paul a call to see how we had got on. As soon as I heard his voice, I knew something wasn't right.

'We only got two, and one is a load of rubbish from Pierse,' Paul said. We had worked hard on Pierse to buy the site, because they were normally strong buyers for this kind of product. They were also ex-clients of Paul from Anglo, and I think their low-ball offer hurt him a little.

'What was the real one like?' I asked, feeling very nervous.

'Not quite there – twenty-eight million euro,' Paul said. 'We'll go to work on them.'

'That's a great price,' I said. 'Don't spook them.'

The bid was from Ascon, not usually a player in this market: they were contractors rather than developers, but it looked as if they were making the transition. They had the backing of a rich Dutch parent company and this gave them firepower in the market. Thankfully, they had fully completed the tender contract at €28 million so they were bound into the deal.

Where have all the builders gone? I wondered, after I'd put down the phone. I slowly worked through why we had only had one bid: the builders all had too much land. Nobody needed another site for 150 apartments or offices or anything else.

We accepted the Blackpitts offer at €28 million and moved on to the tender for the Naas Road site. I was a lot more nervous about that one. It was a pretty marginal location, and I certainly did not want to build out that scheme.

We had bought the site because the price seemed well below the going rate. The Luas – Dublin's new tram service, which was going to run from Naas Road into the city centre – was the key to the planning: it was going to unlock huge density. Density is great in the city centre where there is demand, but Naas Road might be a different kettle of fish. The whole deal felt way too much like my early days in Tallaght, working for nothing but experience.

On tender day I called Paul. I was expecting bad news this time.

'One tender,' Paul said, with a certain bounce in his voice.

'How much?' I asked.

'What do you think would be a good price?' Paul asked.

'Anything is a good offer, but I hope more than thirty million euro,' I said, knowing Paul was happy and the price must be OK.

'Thirty-seven point five million. How's that?' Paul had bought the Naas Road site, and this was his first deal to sell for a profit. He was very keen to earn his stripes as a developer, and this €20 million profit was certainly a great way to start.

'Well done. Wow. Who paid that?' I asked, getting worried. The price was where we had pitched it, but I was surprised we had hit it. I wanted to make sure that it was a good bid from somebody who could pay the balance.

'Nevills,' Paul answered, in an even happier tone. We had a real bid from real people. The Nevills were low-profile developers from Wexford and they were loaded.

'No problem getting paid, then. Well done,' I said.

I sat back into my chair and let out a huge sigh of relief. We had done it. We had sold the two sites for a combined profit of €35 million. We had a queue of delirious investors, flush with profits and waiting to go again.

I had a friend with €100,000 in the Naas Road deal and I was very happy to have made him money.

'You're a genius, Simon,' he said to me, when I called him with the news. 'I've had money with Morgan Stanley for years and they never made me anything. Then I give it to you and you make me over a hundred per cent.'

'No problem. Don't spend it all,' I said.

'I want to give it to you again. You just tell me where,' my friend said, keen to get the same kind of success on another deal.

'Hold tight for now and I'll call you if I see a good one,' I said. I never did call him with another deal. I never saw another deal where I could be sure his money was safe. I don't like losing money, and I certainly don't want to lose a friend's.

Selling those two deals had been a lot tougher than I'd planned, and I knew that the market was in trouble. We were running out of buyers.

6. The Dawn of the Mega-deal

We gained an early-mover advantage by adopting the other-people's-money model in 2005, but it didn't last long. Quinlan Private had been quietly running property syndicates for a number of years with very little competition, but within twelve months of our entry into that sector of the business the pitch was very busy. The arrival of the stockbrokers, led by Davy and Goodbody, had brought a lot of new investors and money into the property business.

The early days, when money was a constant brake on the wheels of a deal, were well behind us. Debt was now available in many guises, and the equity was only a few phone calls away. Banks were piling into the country and opening up their credit lines to property developers and investors. We had never had it so good.

Small deals were being bid up by small developers who were looking to get involved in anything property-related. It seemed to me that the only way to play the game was to move up the value chain into the really big deals. RQB had given me the ammunition to compete in that market, and I also had the energy of Paul and the RQB team to push me forwards. I put away my worries about the market and blindly pressed on.

In early 2005 the market was applying pressure to Jurys Doyle Hotel Group to unlock the development potential in their property portfolio. The company had traded on the stock market for a number of years, but the constant buying of the shares by property-focused investors had begun to drive up the price. The market believed that Jurys Hotel in Ballsbridge was not trading at a sufficient level of profit to justify keeping it. The returns on a Dublin 4 apartment development would greatly exceed any profit that the hotel could generate. The company defended its position, by referring back to its founder P. V. Doyle. PV did not sell things: he held on to them and, over time, they kept rising in value.

As the year progressed, the pressure continued to build. The core hotel trade of Jurys was being battered by new hotel openings. Developers and investors had been very busy building them, driven by demand and tax breaks. Hotel tax breaks were even better than the designated-area tax breaks we had availed ourselves of in Tallaght and Smithfield; by their nature, they were available only in marginal areas. The hotel tax allowances were different. To get the tax break, all you had to do was build a hotel and trade anywhere in Ireland. This had driven an enormous amount of hotel development, and the new supply was squeezing Jurys. They had stopped developing new hotels in Ireland and embarked on a UK expansion trail.

The market wanted the land in Ballsbridge to be sold for two reasons: first, to remove all those hotel bedrooms from the system, thus improving the profits on new bedroom stock; second, to get the site on to the market for the developers to fight over. It seemed that everybody wanted a piece of Ballsbridge, and would pay to get it.

A large residential scheme in Ballsbridge was a dream you were scared to contemplate, in case it ever happened. Large parcels of prime land rarely came up for sale in great locations; when they did, it had always paid to push out the boat.

The allure of Ballsbridge was like that of diamonds: we all know they're common, yet we buy them as though they're rare. People paid too much to live in Ballsbridge, but they paid and that was what counted. I had been brought up in Ballsbridge. Yes, it was nice, and close to town, but beyond that it was just an address. The down-side for me, growing up there, was the people, who seemed to think they were better than everybody else. But as a developer I was happy to feed that myth, and sell those people lots of new apartments to buy for their children. Buying for little Max or Saoirse was the name of the game for rich parents, and a successful development in Ballsbridge meant simply extracting the maximum price from all those parents. Without the support of rich parents, nobody would be able to afford the prices we would need to charge to justify a deal.

As the pressure mounted on Jurys, the stock price began to rise. Steve and I noticed this, but our little share fund was still very long on Anglo, and Anglo was performing great. There was no need for us to play with a small-cap company like Jurys. That did not deter others, however, and the share register began to bulge with new names. After months of pressure, and a hostile takeover bid by the Precinct consortium, the will of the Doyle family was broken and the board voted to let the site go to the market.

In May 2005, it was put up for sale by tender through CBRE and the game was on. Until then, I had been interested in the site but not 100 per cent committed to bidding for it. I had lots of deals on the go and I certainly did not need any more work. That said, if the game was on I had to play; and once I made that decision I was going to play to win. It would be a test of the new RQB model because of its scale. The equity required would be enormous. Anybody backing us on this deal would be taking a view on Ballsbridge and its exceptional prices.

The site was pitched into the market with a guide price of about €150 million, and I immediately knew that was way off the mark: €200 million plus was the name of the game, and the only question was two hundred and what? We quickly settled on HKR Architects and the Smithfield team. Dublin Corporation was very happy with Smithfield, and had granted us a huge density there. To win in Ballsbridge, we would need some of Paddy's planning magic to max out the density.

Density could be maximized through a mixture of site coverage – building on as much of the site as possible – and building height, and the height of the existing Jurys Hotel was a useful precedent. On the opposite side of Lansdowne Road, Hume House was also a tall building by Dublin standards. That got us bullish about the prospects of delivering high density. Jerry Ryan from HKR began sketching a scheme and the picture gradually came together.

Paddy worked on the plans with Jerry and they discussed the aesthetic of the site. They wanted to make a difference in Ballsbridge, whereas I just wanted the density number to plug into my model. The key driver in this deal would be the number and value of the apartments. Because of the unusually high land costs, and the unusually high prices the developer would be able to charge for the apartments, the cost of the construction was of relatively little relevance in my profitability calculations; I built in the largest budget I had ever estimated to ensure that we delivered a high-spec scheme with all the bells and whistles. This deal would be won by spending money, rather than cutting corners.

The site was about five acres – less than an acre larger than the Smithfield site. We had achieved almost 900,000 square feet in Smithfield – a plot ratio of nearly five, which was our target for Ballsbridge.

'We basically need to transplant Smithfield to Ballsbridge,' I told Paddy, when I showed him my model.

I kept running and rerunning the numbers while I waited for the call from Jerry with the plot ratio. Every square foot mattered; every additional apartment made a big difference to the numbers.

While the design progressed, Aidan Marsh of Beauchamps went through the normal legal process. The title for the site was clean, and our queries were minor. The plot-ratio figure was the key and we waited. Five was my hope, but we would not progress until Jerry was happy.

The deal was too big for RQB to finance on its own so I brought in a partner on the bid. I selected the McCormacks because of all our other deals together and the assets we jointly owned. 'If we win this, we'll need a big equity release, and we can get it from the assets we hold with Alanis,' I told Paul, justifying my selection. As well as raising equity from other investors we would need to invest a large amount of our own money in this deal. The only real source would be an equity release on our property portfolio.

The deal was a fifty-fifty joint venture between RQB and Alanis. The McCormacks agreed to bring in Anglo's private bank to fund their half. We hoped that having Anglo Private on board – and, by extension, access to their clients – would give us an edge on the competition.

Anglo was the only bank for a deal like this. Because all the big developers were having a run, we kept it in the dark about the numbers. The tender called for a bank draft of €5 million and that was all we needed from Anglo to get up and running. One phone call, just to tell them who I was bidding with so they could fill in the loan letter, was enough. If we were successful, there would be mountains of money required, but that could wait until after the bid.

I was in a meeting one day when I had a call from Jerry. I stepped out to take it.

'We're pretty confident that four can be achieved,' Jerry said. 'Run with that.'

'Why less than Smithfield?' I asked, seeing if we could push it a little.

'The trees along the boundary are a problem and we think we'll be forced to step down the buildings beside Lansdowne Road,' Jerry answered. In other words, he didn't think we'd be able to build as tall on that side of the site as we'd originally hoped.

The buildings on the opposite side of Lansdowne Road were three-storey Georgian houses, a mixture of private homes and B-and-Bs. Jerry was worried that they'd make it impossible for us to convince the planners to let us build as high as we wanted. Hume House was a useful precedent but not enough to push too hard. Four was not an ideal number, but I knew that most of the architects in town would come to the same conclusion so I was happy to go with it. Less density might mean higher prices, or so I told myself.

With the density locked at a plot ratio of four, the price was the final number I needed to plug into my model. Ballsbridge was really expensive at that time, but we were not going to win the tender by using existing prices. We had costed about four years of time into the model to allow for the planning application. A planning application like that was certain to go to An Bord Pleanála at least once, and every trip there would take about two years. While the planning application was being decided upon, we would have to pay interest on the bank debt and run a return on the equity. We could also use this time period to allow for rising prices, and this was what I did in forming my final view on the bid number. Prices had to keep rising if it was to work out.

'What's the residential element worth?' Niall McCormack asked, at a meeting where we were reviewing the deal. Alanis

had done their own numbers and we were comparing notes
– a kind of sanity cross-check.

'Twelve hundred and fifty euro per square foot,' I told him.

That would put the price of the average one-bed apartment
at about €750,000 and a standard two-bed would be a cool
€1 million. We planned to build about six hundred of these
apartments.

'The penthouses will fly, so that'll add a bit of extra juice,'
I added. We planned to achieve twice this price per foot for
the few select penthouse and sub-penthouse units, which
would really drive the average price up.

'What does Paddy think?' Niall asked, looking to get some
grey-haired thinking into the equation.

'He wants to buy the top penthouse, so that's a good sign,'
I answered. Ballsbridge was full of people living in extremely
valuable houses, and it was our plan to sell the top apartments
to people like them who wished to downsize from their large,
detached homes. Paddy looked like becoming our first
customer. A large house in Ballsbridge would easily cost
€8 million or more, so selling penthouse apartments for
€3–4 million seemed easy in theory.

We did not need to go into the detail of the unit designs
for the tender, but our plan was to build apartments of 4,000
and 5,000 square feet for the very rich. The largest apartment
in a traditional residential scheme was about 1,500 square feet,
but this was not suitable for a downsizer from a large house
in Ballsbridge.

On the day of the tender, 22 July 2005, Paul and I walked
round to the Alanis boardroom to finalize the number and
sign the tender document, which was a binding contract to
buy the land so we needed all our signatures on it. I also think
we all wanted to sign the document. We hoped it might be
somehow historic.

'Let's get the price up with these boys,' said Paul, with real excitement in his voice. It was the biggest deal that any of us had ever been involved in and we were playing to win.

'We'll get them up, don't worry,' I said. I had spent my career getting partners to up their bid prices on the day of the tender and I was not about to stop now. Paul had me focused on the fees for the deal, and they were enormous. It would also be a landmark deal for RQB.

'What about three hundred million euro?' Paul said, really pushing it.

'Too much, Paul. We're agreed at two hundred and fifty million and I think I can get them to two hundred and sixty,' I replied, picking up the pace as we rounded the corner into Fitzwilliam Square.

The tender was at twelve and we were meeting at ten to review the plans, sign off on the legals, and push the button on the price. We arrived at the Alanis office with time to spare and were taken straight through to the boardroom. I poured a cup of strong black coffee and settled into a seat at the head of the long table. Two rows of empty chairs lined it and Paul was pacing at the back of the room, wondering where everybody was. I was happy to be early and first to the coffee. I was running over the deal in my mind, working out all the angles again and again.

After a few minutes the others arrived and we settled down. Small-talk dominated until the last person arrived and the meeting began. The first item was the legals, and Aidan Marsh opened with a review of the tender and the bidding procedure. I switched off for that part of the meeting because I had been through all of it with him over the past few weeks. I kept rolling over the figures again and again.

€1,250 per square foot meant over €1 billion of sales, and that was a nice easy number to hold in your head. Our bid was going to look expensive, but with over €1 billion in sales, we could push it.

'So, in summary, there are some glitches on the title, but nothing I can't fix given a few years,' Aidan concluded. This was the usual story with legals. Nothing was ever perfect, and everything was fixable. We would need to get the title accepted into Land Registry and this would add a little time. There was also a restriction on building or trading a hotel on the land. We felt that this was not a big issue and that it could not be enforced anyway. We hoped that our plan would have some element of hotel in it. The tax break on a Ballsbridge hotel would be very easy to sell and it would also be a great way to brand the development and add value. We had seen the benefit of this in the IFSC by branding the apartment development at Clarion Quay after the hotel next door. But a hotel was not central to our bid and we decided not to include it as a precondition.

It was almost eleven twenty. The tender delivery address was an upstairs room of the Ulster Bank on Dame Street, which was unusual. It was a twenty-five-minute walk away, so we did not have much time.

'Time's moving on, guys. Let's agree the number,' I said. 'I have to collect the cheque from Anglo on the way down so I need a few extra minutes.' The cheque would be in the lobby waiting for me, but I needed a little time to be completely happy. There was no point rushing to deliver the biggest tender of your life.

'What's in the model?' Alan McCormack asked me.

'I have every number in the model but I think we need to go high on this one. Everybody will be bidding,' I said, stating the obvious. We needed a direct decision on price so I pushed on. 'Two hundred and seventy million euro, plus a little for fun,' I said, putting my price out to the room.

'That's a long way from the guide of a hundred and fifty million,' Niall said, trying to talk me down a little.

'We all know that's bullshit, Niall,' I answered. I'm not sure where they got the €150 million from for the original guide, but nobody thought it had any relevance. 'If we're going for this, we have to go for it. We'll need to push.'

I could see that the lads were nervous. It was always hard to know where to pitch a bid and that's the beauty of the tender process. Nobody knows what the other bidders are thinking; everybody is bidding against themselves. The auction room is transparent and a tender is the exact opposite.

'We can get the equity from Anglo and RQB and it'll be a great deal,' I said. It was like pushing a boulder up a hill. I knew they would give up in the end but they wanted me to work a little. I would have to earn this one.

'Once-in-a-lifetime chance, lads,' Paul said, coming to my aid.

'What's the "and a bit" amount?' Alan asked, getting back to my suggested number.

'My lucky number is two hundred and twenty-one so we'll finish with that,' I said.

'Okay, what about the rest?' he said, nodding.

'I think we need to get a little clear of the two hundred and seventy million so let's say €273,221,000,' I said.

'Ouch,' said Alan, recoiling a little.

I got up, walked around the room and stood behind him. I put my hands on his shoulders and began to massage them firmly. 'Come on, Alan, this is what we do,' I said, pressing hard. 'We're developers.' I could feel him coming around.

'I don't want to win by too much,' Alan said, getting comfortable with the decision but hoping to avoid embarrassment.

'We won't, I can tell,' I said. 'We'll not be alone on this one.' Winning a tender is a great feeling but you never want to win by too much. A large winning margin indicates that you have been spooked by the ghosts of the tender process. The last 10 per cent of any bid is almost always gut instinct. It's easy to make a set of numbers work for a price around a 10 per cent swing, so you have to rely on your instinct. Mine told me that we had to go really high here to have a chance.

Aidan Marsh got out his pen and filled in the price on the tender form. He had brought along a gold pen to sign with but I preferred my Bic biro. I signed for RQB and Alan signed for Alanis, and we were on our way.

'I'd love to stay and chat but we've got to fly,' I said, standing up. Paul Pardy got up and we left together, clutching the tender documents.

'Good luck,' was the shout from the room as we left.

We took off at a firm pace towards Anglo to collect the cheque.

'Well done, Simon, brilliant job,' Paul said. I think he had been nervous about the McCormacks. They projected themselves in Anglo as a conservative group, so Paul probably assumed that this was how they were. In truth, behind the conservative front, they were the same as us: deal addicts.

The cheque was waiting in the lobby of Anglo Irish Bank with my name on the envelope. Stephen Collier from my lending team was standing beside the reception desk, waiting for me with a smile. 'Good luck,' he said, as we left the bank. A lot of people are involved in every bid and everyone on the team enjoys the excitement of the deal.

'Did you give out many cheques?' I asked him, as I headed for the door.

'Just a few – five, I think,' he answered.

That was interesting: five Anglo clients were bidding for the site. There was a secondary market going around town, speculating how many bids would be lodged for the site. Eight to ten was the consensus, which was unheard of for a deal of this size.

'Let's go the nice way,' I said to Paul, and we headed down Grafton Street past all the shoppers. It was busy, and it was fun, walking through the crowds with a €5 million bank draft burning a hole in my pocket. We were a little early so we slowed down. The trick with a tender is to deliver it at eleven fifty-nine and not a minute sooner. People would be positioned to see who was delivering, and most would use a solicitor or some unknown person. Paul and I were going to walk in and let everybody see that it was us bidding. We never wanted to hide.

I delivered the document.

'How many are in?' we asked the solicitor, who was signing the receipt.

'You are number seven,' she said, pointing to the receipt where our number was written. We took this to be a good sign – the number was lower than we'd expected, and being seventh seemed lucky.

Paul and I floated back to the office and waited to hear some news. Our spirits were high and we felt we had the knockout number on the page.

Later that afternoon I received an SMS message from Neil Callanan of the *Sunday Business Post*. 'Any word?'

I called him back. I didn't have any word on the bid and I thought he might know more than I did. This deal had generated pages of speculation in the media, where it was being portrayed as a competition for dominance in Dublin – and they were desperate to know the winner. Who was the biggest and baddest developer in town? Who had the balls to buy Jurys and become the new anointed king? I told Neil I'd heard nothing yet.

'What did you bid?' he asked me.

'High,' I said.

'How high? Over two hundred million?' he asked.

'Yes, well over,' I said. I couldn't tell him exactly what we'd bid, but I could help him guess, and he might share a bit of his own information. Rumours were swirling around town about the various bids, but I had not heard of anybody near us. There was talk of Pierse at €200 million and somebody else at €220 million. We had put everything on the line in picking our number, and I was beginning to get that lucky feeling.

Neil signed off and we said we would stay in touch and share information. I drove home without hearing anything. I could visualize the tender opening. Each envelope would be opened in order, and the bid would be registered. I knew ours would have made an impression when it was read out, but I did not know if we were on top.

'Could somebody have bid three hundred million?' I asked myself. Dublin was hot but it couldn't be that hot, I thought. On my way home, I pulled into Tesco in Wicklow town to pick up some dinner. As I walked the aisles choosing the various items, my phone buzzed in my pocket. It was a message from Neil: *I hear it's Dunner.* Sean Dunne was at the top of the list.

How much? I replied, not really believing this. Could Sean have done it? He would not have been on my list of major threats prior to the tender. He was a dark horse.

What did you bid? Niall asked again. I felt he had real news but I would need to trade it.

Over €260m, I sent back, leaving a little room for mystery.

He is over €270m. I hear there are three bids very close together was Niall's response. This was tighter than I'd ever imagined possible. Three bids of about €270 million, and then the rest: that's over €1 billion of demand for a site in Ballsbridge. The value on every piece of land in Ballsbridge – including the Berkeley Court Hotel, adjacent to Jurys Hotel and part of the Jurys Doyle group – had just gone into the stratosphere. I already owned a building in Ballsbridge, the old Cablelink headquarters beside Herbert Park. What's that worth? I wondered.

The news became official the next morning: they were dealing with a preferred bidder. No name was mentioned, but we knew it wasn't us. A tender normally remains open for ten days and the sellers can accept any offer so we were all still on tenterhooks. CBRE stayed in touch with me to keep my bid alive while they dealt with Sean Dunne on the details. The main challenge for any bidder was to prove that they had the money. €270 million, plus stamp duty, was a lot to find even in that hot market, and it seemed to be taking Sean a few days longer than Jurys were comfortable with.

I travelled to Belgium with Joanna and the kids to visit some friends, but my phone was on through the weekend. CBRE were sending me updates, and Alan McCormack was sending me bits of information from the Jurys end of the deal: an associate of theirs was a board member, so we had a little news flow through the back channel. The messages were both the same: 'Stay available: we may need to call you.' If Sean stumbled, we were to be on hand to pick up the ball.

In the end, Sean did not stumble and our contract and cheque were returned to us. Sean had won the prize.

This filled me with mixed emotions. It was a competition and I had wanted to win; but when I heard that we'd failed, I was filled with relief. Deep down I did not want the site, because I had enough sites, and I certainly did not want to try to find the €300 million that we would have needed to buy it and pay the stamp duty.

Once Jurys had agreed to sell the site to Sean, a battle began to brew for the rest of the company. Investors had a look at the price paid for Jurys Ballsbridge and began to compute the value of the entire company.

'What's it all worth?' Paddy asked me, a few days after the tender.

I wasn't sure: plc accounts are designed to hide the crown-jewel assets in order to put off unwanted bidders. Jurys were never transparent about their property portfolio valuation, and all of Dublin was now doing the same sums that Paddy and I were doing. The stock price was rising and people were getting ready for the next round. If we could force the company to sell the Jurys site, we could force them to sell the whole lot, and that would keep us busy for a few years to come. The market did not balk at the idea of all that property coming for sale at the one time. The banks were there and ready to fund it.

The frenzy over Jurys shares forced Sean Dunne to defend his position on the deal by acquiring a large stake in the company. He went into the market and spent over €200 million buying shares in Jurys, making sure he had enough votes at the EGM, which had to approve his deal. Interesting new players began to appear on the share register, including Liam Carroll, who took a stake of 10 per cent in the company.

We watched this process from the sidelines as we ran the figures to acquire the whole company. The key to any take-over was the will of the Doyle sisters, who owned nearly a quarter of the shares between them. To gain real control of the plc and get the resolutions passed you needed to own at least 75 per cent of the shares. Banks would not lend the money required unless they could get a charge on the actual property assets of the company. The only way to make this happen was to own more than 75 per cent of the company and take it private.

Running the rule over Jurys and seeing the continuing intensity of demand for property assets, I began to look on our own assets in a different light.

'What would people pay for our stuff?' I said to Paddy.

'Why would we sell?' he replied. 'The tax would be too high.'

It was true that the tax system provided a disincentive to sell. Although stamp duty – at 9 per cent of the purchase price – was legally the responsibility of the buyer, in practice the cost of stamp duty was always subtracted from the price: in effect, the seller paid. Capital gains tax of 20 per cent was then levied on the gain that you would make from selling a building. In a rising market, and in a banking climate where the equity you held could produce enormous leverage for new deals, all the incentives seemed to be stacked against selling.

My unexpected relief at not buying Jurys had opened my eyes to the market. It was crazy, and running with the herd was not the smart thing to do. We had started as a small nimble speedboat all those years ago in Dundrum and Tallaght, and now we had become a supertanker. I might have wanted to turn around and change course, but the ship was too big to stop and the partnership structure we had adopted meant that there were too many captains on board trying to steer it. The ship was now steering itself, and its only course was more of the same.

At this point, we had a portfolio of property that was very valuable and we had assets worth €700 million and debt of over €500 million. Development land was not a large part of our portfolio: it was concentrated in a small number of large sites. I began seriously to consider selling property despite the taxation costs. We carried a large amount of debt and our cash flow was never comfortable due to the drain from property-development expenses. I was getting tired of dealing with the banks, constantly borrowing more money.

If other people were thinking similar thoughts, there was no sign of it in the market. Jurys sparked a wave of deals. The power of OPM, combined with apparently limitless bank facilities, threw a wave of liquidity into the market. Jurys plc continued to spit out sites and people continued to snap them up. Sean Dunne stepped up and purchased the Berkeley Court Hotel on similar terms to the Jurys deal. He continued his expansion in Ballsbridge by paying record money for Hume House and part of the AIB Bank Centre opposite the RDS. He made those deals without a lot of competition from the market, because by then he was seen as the winner in Ballsbridge. (One man stepped in his way on the Veterinary College site, which adjoins Jurys: Ray Grehan set a new record price for land, paying over €80 million per acre.) We did not bid for any of those deals, because I could no longer do the maths to make them work. Also I had lost the hunger for them. My appetite was sated.

I watched these spiralling prices from the sidelines, and returned to the core focus of progressing our existing projects. It was not as exciting as bidding for new land, but it would pay the bills.

Another developer who had recently discovered OPM was starting to make his mark all over Dublin. Bernard McNamara had been handed the keys to any site on the market, with Davy stockbrokers providing the equity, and he went on a monster spending spree. Every deal seemed to be bought by either Sean or Bernard; it was as if the Dublin market had become a duopoly.

In early 2007 Bernard bought the Burlington Hotel for redevelopment at a cost of €288 million. He had previously bought the Allianz office building on Burlington Road for

€100 million. The Allianz land adjoined the hotel at the rear
and along its boundary, and it would provide access to Burlington Road. This would improve the address and add value
to the hotel development. That put the Burlington site in the
same league as the Jurys site in Ballsbridge. There seemed to
be no limit to what developers were willing to pay for large
opportunities in Dublin 4. The deal was backed by Bank of
Scotland (Ireland) (BOSI), who were now happy to lend all
the debt and all the equity to finance property developments;
a great rivalry had built up between them and Anglo – they
had even taken an office similar to Anglo's on St Stephen's
Green, as if to stalk their prey.

When I asked BOSI about their new equity lending
policy to developers, they told me that for the right deal
they would do all the money, like Anglo. This was a change
again in the market. In the past, banks might have lent you
all the money for a deal, but they would not like to acknowl-
edge this possibility in advance. You had to sweat for the
money and maybe borrow the equity on a different building
for window-dressing purposes. BOSI was the first bank to
front up about making 100 per cent possible. They had
decided that the risk was about the same, whether they were
lending 75 per cent or 100 per cent towards a deal, but that
the profits on the 100 per cent loan could be much higher.
Armed with their money, Bernard McNamara could pay
almost anything for the Burlington deal.

Ulster Bank had funded the Jurys deal and BOSI had
funded the Burlington. Anglo had become noticeable by their
absence in the large deals. They had a new policy: 'No new
clients and no new deals,' was the mantra. The market had
hit a number of new highs, and Anglo felt that it had got a
little frothy. They were now happy to step aside and let the
other banks do some development lending while they turned

their gaze to other opportunities. In 2006, for example, they funded the management buyout of Davy stockbrokers from Bank of Ireland.

In late 2006, around the time the Irish Glass Bottle site in Ringsend came up for sale, I was in Anglo discussing the market and various loans. 'We're not going to fund it so don't even ask,' Joe McWilliams told me, before I'd even mentioned the Glass Bottle deal.

'I wasn't going to ask, Joe, so don't worry. It's one too many,' I replied.

'Yeah. Credits have reviewed it and decided to let this one pass,' Joe said.

This decision did not surprise me. I had seen Anglo close down credit for development land since the Jurys deal.

The Glass Bottle site was brought to market by South Wharf plc and put up for tender by Stephen Cassidy of Hamilton Osborne King. Stephen had bought and sold a few deals for me and he was straight on the phone once he got the agency. 'Will you have a go, Simon, with RQB?' he asked me. RQB was riding high and he knew we could do the deal and raise the money.

'No, it's too far down the quay and it's too much money,' I told him. The site was stuck in a no man's land between the very successful South Docks area and Sandymount. HOK were going to try to sell the deal as a pukka Dublin 4 development site on the back of the Ballsbridge deals, but I was not buying this and I couldn't believe that the market would buy it either.

South Wharf had won the right to sell the land during a court battle with Dublin Port, from which they held a long-term lease. A loophole existed in the Landlord and Tenant Act, which allowed leaseholders to acquire the freehold of their site for a small payment once they had made certain

improvements under their lease. The law was a throwback
to the old days of absentee landlords and impoverished
tenants, and we were very careful in all our commercial leases
to avoid getting stung by it. The Irish state and semi-state
sector were not as diligent in that, and under this loophole
South Wharf plc had established ownership on two-thirds
of the land, with Dublin Port owning the other third. It was
a great coup for South Wharf, and the company's share price
had been rising to reflect the value of the land. For a while,
the share price was directly linked with the land value and
you could, in effect, bet on the value of the site by buying or
selling the shares. (Not many of the company's shares were
traded, so you could not buy the site that way.)

The Dublin Docklands Development Authority were very
keen to do a deal with a developer on the site, and they asked
Paddy if we'd bid with them on the land. That was a great
telephone call to receive: it showed how we had progressed
from outsiders in the docklands to preferred insiders. But we
did not let this new status get to our heads and we declined
their offer.

'Don't you know the party's over?' Paddy said to them,
when he turned down their offer.

In the end, Bernard McNamara showed up again, with a
knockout offer of €412 million. The market got a glimpse of
the power of syndication in that deal when it became public
that Bernard would own a third of the site for an investment
of just €5 million. For a while, it looked like a good deal for
Bernard because he would get a very large building contract
out of it, but then the details of the structure began to emerge.

'He's given Davy's a PG [personal guarantee] on the equity
plus a seventeen per cent return,' Niall McFadden told me,
when we were discussing the deal in an RQB board meeting.
'It's crazy,' he said – and it was. You need a lot of confidence

to sign any personal guarantee, and giving one with a 17 per cent coupon return pushes the outer limits of logic.

The rate of change in the property business was accelerating all the time and the changes were giving more ammunition to developers to pay more for land. The days of simple debt and equity were well behind us and stockbrokers and bankers were driving up the price of everything. RQB had successfully sold two sites into this boom and we had a large group of very happy investors. The purchase of Sawgrass in 2006 for $220 million had opened us up to a long list of established professional investors and we were confident about our client base and our ability to raise cash for deals from these clients. Paul Pardy was out looking for a new deal for the business, and we had skipped from Dublin to London.

All through the 2000s I had made regular trips to London to take a look at deals, but nothing had really grabbed me. London is a difficult market to compete in for the large deals because of the number of players. The Irish had had a strong run with a number of deals funded by Irish banks, but to get those you'd had to pay what I called the 'Paddy premium'. All the London agents were happy to sell to the Irish once you'd paid the premium. I was not happy to pay it so I had never bought any development property in London.

Paul Pardy was working hard on getting a deal, and his black book of contacts was being exhausted in that endeavour. When he got the chance to form a joint venture with Sean Mulryan's Ballymore on sixteen acres of the London Docklands he jumped at the chance. The deal was called Unex and he brought it back to the RQB board with great excitement: he had shaken hands on a deal to buy 50 per cent of the site from Ballymore based on an initial price of £190 million, rising to £240 million once certain planning milestones were achieved.

From the start I hated the deal. I felt the site was too far down the river to be worth the money he had agreed to pay. I had bought six apartments in a better location, closer to Canary Wharf, and I had not paid anything like the price we needed to achieve to make the numbers work. At these prices, I wanted to be a seller rather than a buyer. But I felt we had to let Paul have a go. A lot of deals were started and looked at by RQB only to fade away, and I hoped that this would be one of those deals.

Niall McFadden had increased his stake in RQB to take technical control of the business. This had cost him €1 million, and we had stepped aside to allow him to take majority control. I hoped that he would control Paul on this one. Development funding was getting a lot more difficult as the US market began to unravel, and I thought that might also be a problem on this deal. I hoped that somebody or something would block it. I did not want to be the one to try to put the brakes on.

The deal progressed through the summer of 2007 as the details were ironed out. RQB had agreed to purchase the 50 per cent share of the site, subject to finance, which in effect gave us an option on it without a legal obligation. By late 2007, the deal was still progressing and Bank of Ireland had agreed to fund it by issuing a non-binding term sheet on the finance. On the back of that term sheet, the equity sale team had mobilized and were getting ready to raise the £55 million of equity, which was the amount that the deal would need.

The sub-prime mortgage market in the USA had begun to go off the rails in mid-2007, and the impact on banks and property was beginning to ripple back to Europe and Ireland. At the time, Anglo was trying to get all their clients to buy interest-rate swaps to hedge off the risk of interest-rate rises, and I was getting regular phone calls from their swaps desk quoting rates to me.

'They're all too high,' I told the swaps guy, when he went through the prices. Earlier in the year, we had been strongly encouraged by Anglo to buy some swaps and I did not want any more. My gut told me that something was going to go wrong in the markets, and that rates were going to come down.

'It's all too quiet,' I told the swaps guy. 'When it's this quiet, I don't trust it.'

In trading the markets with Steve, I had seen the speed at which a crisis could emerge. We had survived the dotcom crash and all the pain that had caused the world markets.

Following a meeting with Anglo in the summer of 2007, I had got on the phone to Steve as I walked out of the bank. 'Sell all the Anglo shares,' I said, as he answered the phone.

'Why? Anything happened?' he asked.

'Nothing really, just a feeling,' I said. 'I just met with them on a few deals and they were a real pain in the arse. If they're squeezing me, they must be squeezing everybody.'

Steve immediately sold our whole long position in the bank. We got a price of just over €17 per share, which was just off their record high. I was happy to be out of the position. A few days later I picked up the phone and rang my mum. 'Hi, Mum. You need to sell your Anglo shares now,' I said to her, without sounding panicked. They had now fallen below €17 and were pointing south.

'Why? I met David Drumm last week and he said they were doing great,' she replied.

'Don't believe him. You can always buy back the shares when they fall,' I told her, knowing she would not be buying them back. She had invested €100,000 in them at about €12 each so she had done well. I did not want her to get burned. Happily, she took the advice and sold them.

But while my gut was telling me something was wrong,

Paul was pushing ahead with Unex and nobody – myself included – seemed to be pulling him back.

The initial loan offer on Unex from Bank of Ireland had our normal limited-recourse RQB terms. On the back of that loan offer, RQB had borrowed €10 million from National Irish Bank (NIB) and used the money to pay a booking deposit on the site. The €10 million was not fully committed to the deal as a deposit until the banking was in place, and Niall had gone to great lengths to get that clearly in the contract. We still had an option to walk away if the banking became a problem.

At that stage, I had only shared my doubts about the deal with Paddy. RQB had become a political animal once I had stepped aside to let Niall and Paul run the show. I was still a director and I still advised on development land and strategy, but Niall was firmly in charge of the overall business. I was worried about Paul's hunger for this deal.

I was driving up from Wicklow in late 2007 with Paddy and we were discussing various projects. I decided to bite the bullet and call Paul about another deal we were doing, with a view to discussing Unex. I had agreed to sell one of my sites in Kilkenny to RQB for a profit of €2 million, and they still owed me that money, although the purchase had been completed a few weeks ago. The fourth quarter of every year was always tight for cash and I wanted to make sure that RQB could pay in December.

'It'll be fine. I'll have it sorted,' Paul replied, with stress in his voice. I pushed on, asking if he'd run the Kilkenny payment by Niall. Without Niall's sign-off I wouldn't get paid. I needed Paul to get this done, so I tried to encourage him along the path.

'Don't talk about Niall,' Paul snapped, and then he was off on a tirade about Niall, Paddy, me and the whole world.

I saw my chance. 'The bank have changed the funding on Unex, Paul,' I said. 'We have to walk away.'

'Walk away from Ballymore? Are you mad? I shook their hand,' Paul screamed.

'Paul, the price is too high,' I said, in my calmest voice. 'Are you watching the market? It's going to tank.' I continued: 'Ballymore are big boys so they can take it. The deal is subject to finance and we do not have finance. We can walk away.'

'You don't understand,' he told me, with a quiver in his voice, which ended the call.

I turned to Paddy, who had overheard the whole exchange. The call had not been on speaker but Paul was loud enough for anybody nearby to hear.

'Something's wrong here,' I said, as we drove past Stillorgan. Paul was way too edgy.

'Let me talk to him,' Paddy said. He could calm down almost any situation, and he was probably the only person Paul would listen to.

Over the next few days it became clear what the problem was. The RQB board had begun to look at the details of the Unex deal and the other directors had become increasingly uneasy. Then the bombshell landed. 'Paul committed us contractually. We're stuck in the deal,' David Kelly told me, when we met in the office.

'He what?' I said, with real horror.

'He waived the finance clause so we're totally bollixed,' David said.

'When?' I asked.

'A few weeks ago,' David said.

Now everything became clear to me. Paul was burning up inside. We were now fully on the line for £120 million, and we needed to raise the equity to repay the €10 million we had borrowed from NIB as an equity bridge overdraft within three months.

His deal to pay me €2 million in Kilkenny was now gone, caught up in the same storm as Unex and the whole of RQB. All deals were frozen, until we decided what to do on Unex. This deal had put the whole company at risk, and my €2 million now fell to the back of a long line.

We were short on the equity for the Unex deal by more than £20 million and the market was shutting down. Bank of Ireland were firming up on their personal-guarantee requirements and that was adding fuel to the fire. Niall and Paul could hardly be in the same room, and I just wanted to be away from it all.

We had to push on and try to make the best of a bad situation. We completed the purchase, scraping through on the equity fundraising with a bridging loan from Ballymore, leaving the £10 million overdraft in place. Ballymore certainly needed to sell the site because they rolled over on almost everything to get the deal done. Once it was progressing and they were getting paid, they were happy. From their point of view, it was a great deal.

For us it was not so good. We were stuck in a mega-deal that we should never have done, all because of one signature on one letter signed by Paul. For now, we pushed on optimistically because it was all we could do. We were personally on the hook for the €10 million overdraft and we had been forced at the last minute by Bank of Ireland to provide personal guarantees for up to £10 million of the interest on the debt. Aside from these personal exposures, the deal had poisoned RQB and all of its potential.

7. Staring at the Exit

Christmas is a terrible time in the property business. As a developer you are at the very top of a large and hungry supply chain, and below you are hundreds of people wanting to make sure they have enough money to relax over the holidays. You can time the start of the financial run-in from the first corporate lunch on the first day of December. It's the same every year. Once December starts, your whole focus needs to be on getting deals completed and loans drawn down. You need to generate the finance to make it to January. The property industry's Christmas starts on 24 December, and it generally runs through to mid-January. In any business that is a long time to have no revenue. To make matters even worse, all the bankers disappear so their money dries up as well.

The hungry suppliers begin to look for the money during the first weeks of December. The flood of gifts starts then as well. 'Obscene' is the only word that I can use to describe it. The hampers would pile up in the reception area alongside cases of wine and bottles of Midleton whiskey. We would open the hampers to see what was fresh and what would keep until Christmas. I would share the bounty with the office team and anybody who walked into the building. If you came for a meeting, you might leave with a smoked salmon or a box of chocolates. I wanted to make sure that everybody got something nice, from the cleaning ladies to the accountants. My goal was to close the office on 24 December with everybody paid and clutching a case of wine to bring home. As the

Celtic Tiger grew, so did the gifts, and Christmas 2006 was the record year.

With the gifts piling up in the lobby, I laid out my cash plan for the run-in, and I really wanted to nail it that year. I was going away for two weeks to our ski resort in Italy, Pragelato, and I wanted to turn off the phone and really enjoy my time there. We've spent enough money building the place, so I'd better enjoy it, was my main thought.

You always needed a couple of million euro handy to make Christmas an easy affair. Invoices would come out of everywhere, and people would arrive with their sorry stories about how they needed to be paid. It was like the world was going to end on the twenty-fifth , and that there would be no money at all in January or ever again. Nobody could see past Christmas Eve, and I couldn't wait to get to it.

By now I knew the drill well. I always tried to have a reserve of cash, because somebody would inevitably let me down. I had learned this lesson the hard way in previous years. A sure thing would always turn into a maybe thing, and would then end up as nothing.

I was certain that December 2006 was going to be an easy one because I had lined up a nice profit payout from an apartment development in the South Docks called Gallery Quay. It was a scheme we had built in partnership with Alanis, and Pierse Contracting. The profits had been made and they were sitting in a bank account waiting to be shared out. We were the biggest shareholders in the deal at over 40 per cent, and the profit distribution was going to provide me with some real money.

I flew out on 20 December leaving David Knowles in the office to close out the year-end. David was part of the finance team, and he was the man who knew where all the money was. One of his great skills was always to have a hidden reserve

of cash in case I ever needed it. He also dealt with the creditors, working out who would get what at Christmas time.
All the cheques were written, and we were waiting to lodge
the profit cheque from Gallery Quay, which was over €2
million. The idea of having that resting in the bank over
Christmas gave me a very comfortable feeling as I boarded
the plane in Dublin for Milan. The snow and the Alps
beckoned.

I would have preferred to lodge the cheque prior to leaving, but Alan McCormack and I had agreed on the
distribution earlier in the month and I was confident it would
arrive.

The last day to lodge a cheque was Friday, 22 December.
By Friday morning, Alan had not sent over the money and
he was not picking up his phone. David Knowles had a list
of cheques he had sent out to the various suppliers, and they
were all going to hit the account over the holidays. The last
thing I wanted was the bank on the phone complaining about
limits and the like. I finally got hold of Alan at about two
o'clock and he acted as if the money were irrelevant.

'What's the rush? Let's do it in January,' he said, trying to
sound nonchalant.

'Alan, stop pissing about,' I said. He always tried to play it
too cool. 'You agreed this and I need it. I'm sending David
around now to collect the money.'

'I need to run it by the DDDA,' Alan said, trying to buy
more time.

'Alan, it's my money,' I said, feeling very annoyed. 'Just
write the cheque. There is no more time. We agreed this
ages ago.'

'OK, send David round.' He'd finally relented, as if he was
granting me some special favour.

I sent an email to David and he went to the Alanis offices

to collect the cheque. He was pretty relaxed about the close call because he was used to me pulling money from hats when we really needed it. It was different for me – inside I was churning. I switched off the phone, formally announcing the start of my Christmas to myself because nobody else was around. Christmas could begin only when all the money was sorted. I walked out into the snowy square outside the reception area of our apartment and looked up at the mountains. *What is this bullshit?* I thought. *I should be enjoying myself and this is not fun any more.*

All through 2006 I had felt different about the business. I longed to get free of the banks and the partners. That year RQB had partially allowed this to happen and we had generated profits in the company of at least €10 million. RQB was better than traditional property development because we took the profits and we could spend them. They were real, unlike the paper profits of traditional property development. In RQB, there were no lingering relationship problems with the banks. Every deal was well capitalized and could stand alone to succeed or fail. But outside RQB we still had a huge and unwieldy web of assets and cross-securities that I was finding difficult to manage.

Since 2002, when I had moved with Joanna and our growing family to Wicklow, my perspective on the world had been changing. No longer living in Dublin, I began to observe the Dublin property market as an outsider. Country living had started as a joke to my partners in Dublin, but the air and rich atmosphere had changed me. Staying at home with our twins after their birth in early 2006 had changed me even more. I had enjoyed the time away from the business.

By the end of 2006, the change in my life had brought about a raging need for change in my business. If I could have walked away from it that day in the Italian Alps, I would have. In the past I had talked with Anglo about walking away, and their faces had turned pale. 'You're joking,' they would say, with worried smiles. 'We need people like you, Simon, to get things done. You can't leave.'

'Well, I don't want to be that person any more. I want to change,' I said.

Versions of this conversation took place a few times with various lenders in the bank and generally resulted in them giving me an easy run with some money for a while. Money was their fix-all.

Walking around the square in Italy, looking up at the Alps, I felt certain that I wanted out. But how could I get out? The business had depended for years on my ducking and diving around money. We constantly needed to generate lots of cash to keep the projects going. If I was going to be able to walk away into the sunset, I had to get cash into the business, so that somebody else could take it on.

We had a name for this kind of cash: 'fuck-you money'. Once you had enough of it, you could do anything. As Kieran Duggan in Anglo would say, 'When you're tight for money, you need me, and that's the way I like it.' This might have suited Anglo but it didn't suit me.

I knew now that we were just pawns in the business, operating on behalf of banks. They always needed somebody to front the project, and I suited that role.

With the cheque from Gallery Quay in the bank, Christmas 2006 had proven to be one of our best from a financial point of view. We had broken no limits and everybody had got paid. I returned home in January to put my plan into action during this period of relative calm. I needed cash and the only way to get it was to sell assets. I was going to break the golden rule of property. I had been preparing quarterly statements of affairs for the banks since the mid-1990s. These documents had grown and grown, and I wasn't secretive about the information they contained; I would joke with the banks that you could probably find my statement of affairs on Google if you really looked. There was never any mystery about what we owned and what we owed. By the end of 2006 the document listed more than a hundred separate properties, and it was from this list that I began to hatch my plan.

In a property boom, people who own property hate to sell it. There are normally lots of buyers bidding for a small pool of assets from a small number of sellers, and this is the dynamic that drives prices continually up. My instinct was to sell the whole lot and start again with a large pile of money, but I knew that was not possible. Our tentacles spread too wide into too many partnerships for that to be possible. We had over €700 million of gross assets, but to realize this, more than €3 billion of property would need to be sold – and a lot of partners would have to agree to the sales. Even then, at the peak of the market, annual turnover in the whole commercial property market for Ireland was only €1 billion, so I could not press a button on my computer and hit 'sell', as I could with my CFDs. I really wished I could, though.

Selling property seemed to be a lot more difficult than buying it. For every property I wanted to sell, there was a problem that needed to be fixed. We were generally waiting to get planning permission, or a new tenant, or there was some other annoying detail standing in the way of a quick sale. Some of the large trophy properties would have been ready to go, but putting them on the market at that stage was not an option with our partners. Despite all these obstacles, I drove on and slowly generated a list of assets for sale.

The apartments I owned myself – about seven units in Dublin and London – were first on the block and I hoped to generate about £500,000 in clear cash from those sales.

Even selling these assets was not a simple exercise, so I outsourced this job to a business partner who lived in London; he cleaned up the units and got them ready for sale. Over a period of about six months, the money rolled in. My brother had similar properties and I advised him to start selling. Even parting with these small properties prompted howls of complaint from some quarters.

'Why are you selling? You're mad,' was the standard line.

'You're just going to pay tax and incur cost,' was another.

'Warren Buffett never sells,' was the final putdown.

I pushed on regardless with what I called the €50-million plan: at the end of this process, I hoped we would have €50 million of funds on deposit to do with as we pleased, and that this money would allow me to walk away from the business. The walk-away part was still my secret, and I shared it only with Joanna. I doubt even she believed me. Nobody ever walked away.

The real beauty of the €50-million plan was that we did not have to sell any of the trophy office building or development deals. It allowed us to generate the money by selling off the small assets we hardly knew we owned – bits of pubs, and small sites we couldn't process efficiently. I would have loved to include some of the big deals and maybe turn it into a €100-million plan, but I knew that Paddy and the other partners would not go for this.

I had a few office buildings in the plan, but none of the large ones in the Dublin core. I explained to Paddy that, at the end of this process, we would look more like a safe old pension fund with a few large development sites. Security and comfort beckoned. I hoped our development business could be run and expanded through RQB, which seemed to be a much more secure platform than traditional development.

I quickly discovered that even the small sales were causing

disruption with our partners. Most of them seemed to believe that property prices would rise for ever, or that one more planning application would unlock huge additional value. A little more time was always the answer. But the values were high enough for me, so I pushed on.

Arena Road in Sandyford was an office block we had developed a few years previously with Allied Irish Investment Managers (AIIM). We owned the building on a fifty-fifty joint venture with them and shared our 50 per cent with the Flynn family. The property was at the top of my list because the market in Sandyford had got very hot since the Beacon development there had successfully sold out. Sandyford was trading at €25 million per acre and our office building was on more than an acre of land in a strategic location. A large land bank was being built up by the Alken brothers, and their site adjoined our building. In addition to the development potential, the building generated about €1.4 million per annum in rent, which would provide a buyer with income while they worked up a redevelopment plan.

I floated the idea of selling the building with Paddy and John Flynn, and met with initial resistance from Paddy.

'It's a great building. Why would we sell it?' he asked.

'Because it's a nice building and it's in Sandyford and we can get paid,' I answered.

'Why not gear up on it? What would Anglo lend?' Paddy asked. That was exactly what I was trying to avoid. I didn't want to borrow more money. I wanted to sell. Selling was emotionally different. The building would be gone and would never come back. Gear-ups generated money, all right, but they did not clear the desk. Nothing was as clean as a sale.

'I'll talk to John, see what he thinks,' Paddy said, as we closed off the call.

After a few weeks' going back and forth, we agreed to sell.

We now had to convince the pension fund to follow, and that proved to be another barrier. They did not see any reason to sell. But we were pretty committed to the process by now, so we hard-balled them, insisting that if they didn't want to sell, they'd have to buy out our 50 per cent. That was a strong argument to use with a reluctant partner: if you're not a seller, you're a buyer, so buy us out.

It took about three months from my initial decision to sell the building to persuade everybody to agree and to get the building on the market. We appointed Adrian Truick of HT Meagher O'Reilly to handle the sale. Adrian is very well connected with the institutional buyers and we thought that this deal would go to an investor rather than a developer. €35 million was our target price, and this would have given an investor an initial yield of 4 per cent. That was pretty low for Sandyford, but it priced in the development potential. After a month of marketing and advertising, we reached agreement with the adjoining landowner to sell the property to them. The price was a little soft at €32 million, but we all agreed with it and the deal was on. The loan-to-value ratio on the building was low at about 43 per cent, so the sale was due to generate about €4.5 million for us: not a bad result for an asset that was very low on our radar. The Flynns were set to receive the same amount, and AIIM would get a clear €16 million because they had no debt on their 50 per cent.

We sent out the contracts to the purchasers and waited for the deal to progress. AIIM were managing this process with McCann FitzGerald solicitors so we let them drive it on.

Meanwhile I had let it be known through the agents that we were interested in doing some deals. The message back was always the same: 'What are you selling for? These are great sites.'

'A little bit of trimming and cutting back,' I would say in response.

Next on the block was the Cablelink building, as we used to call it, in Ballsbridge. I'd bought it in partnership with Irish Life Pension Fund in early 2000 for €6.6 million. It was a sweet deal because I got Irish Life to put up €6 million and we received 55 per cent of the development rights to the site in return for our investment of €600,000. Later on this deal went a little sour with Irish Life and we bought out their position, giving them a small profit. ACC provided our consortium with the facility to do this. As Ballsbridge had gone crazy with the frenzied bidding for Jurys and the other sites, I had sat back and happily watched the value of the Cablelink building rise. It occupied half an acre and it was in a prime location, adjoining the Herbert Park Hotel and Herbert Park itself in the heart of Ballsbridge. Our development plan envisaged a large residential tower overlooking the park. We felt that this location had far greater potential than Sean Dunne had on the Jurys site. Planning permission was certainly going to be an issue, and we had leased out the office building in the intervening years, but even if redevelopment was not on the agenda the rental income made it an efficient site to hold.

Despite all of this potential, and the mystique of Ballsbridge, I managed to get our partners to agree to put the site on the market. I appointed CBRE to carry out the sale and we advertised it heavily, with a guide price of €30 million. I was hoping to achieve something over €25 million. This had been our most recent valuation and it equated to the €60 million per acre that Sean Dunne had paid. My partners had set this as an anchor figure below which we would not trade. The bank debt was only €12 million at the time, so this one was looking like a real cash cow. We hoped that the adjoining landowners might bite at the opportunity to expand and improve the Herbert Park Hotel. The public-sale process often has the desired effect of coaxing bids out of people who have been sitting on the fence.

Selling in Sandyford was one thing but selling in Ballsbridge was something different altogether. Word began to filter back to me that the building was not really for sale. I got a phone call from James Mulhall, the agent for the sale. 'What's going on?' James said.

'James, believe me. It is for sale. Ignore the rumours,' I replied.

'Somebody's telling buyers that there's no point bidding. This is not helping,' James answered.

This was my worst nightmare. Somebody in the partnership was saying the sale was not real and that we were only testing the market. 'I've bought and paid for adverts,' I said, trying to make James believe me. 'This is a real sale.' I needed him to convince buyers that it was a real deal. In the end it made no difference. On the day of the tender, we got no serious bids, just a soft offer of €20 million. The deal had been well and truly spiked.

This was not going to be as easy as I had hoped. I was still a long way from €50 million.

'I met Peter Butler today and he mentioned that he might look at Burlington Road,' Paddy said to me, in the office, one day in mid-2007. He passed off this remark as if it did not matter.

'Wow, that would be a great deal,' I answered, trying not to sound too keen. I didn't really believe that we would sell Burlington Road because it was at the top of our deal pile. If I sounded too keen, it might not happen, so I tried to hold back my excitement.

'He asked me to send up the numbers. He's got some new fund which is interested,' Paddy said.

'I'll get them to him,' I said, as I rushed away to get a pack together.

In March 2000 we had tendered £10,221,000 to buy the office building at 6 Burlington Road from Fyffes. That was the first time my magic 221 had been successful in a tender. We felt particularly lucky on the deal because we won the tender by less than £50,000. AIIM were the under-bidders, and they had a very strong interest in the site because they owned the building next door, at 8 Burlington Road, which was occupied by Ark Life.

Shortly after we had won the tender, Paddy had a call to come and sit down with John Bruder, the CEO of AIIM. John really wanted to be part of the redevelopment of Burlington Road and we agreed a fifty-fifty joint venture for the development of the two buildings. We also agreed to try to expand the site to include No. 4. It was a very large piece of property in prime central Dublin, and Burlington Road had always been a great office location.

Within a couple of years we had acquired 4 Burlington Road from Ulster Bank, and I had also done a deal to relocate the ESRI, the one long-term tenant blocking the scheme, to the South Docks. That meant we had the site fully cleared and ready for development. We achieved a very good planning permission for an office building of over 250,000 square feet, and this had caught the eye of Peter Butler.

Peter Butler was the head of Anglo Irish Bank Private, and he was on a mission in 2007 to get access to prime property deals to package for his private clients. His model was pretty simple. Anglo would acquire a prime property asset and they would put in senior debt of about 75 per cent. This would leave an equity requirement of about 25 per cent, and the private bank would lend this money to high-net-worth investors to close out the deal. In effect this was 100 per cent finance, but it was very profitable for the bank because it generated a lot of fees and interest income. The bank could list the deal as 75 per cent funded because the equity loans were in the names of the individuals. Those deals were very popular with investors as well because there was no cash down, and in the past the profits had been high.

Anglo Private was based in Burlington Road too – at No. 1 – and with my pack prepared I arranged to meet Peter at his office there. The deal was going to be a little different from a straight sale. We planned to sell Anglo the completed office building by way of a land and building contract. Anglo wanted to own the finished building, but we needed to sell it to them now to avoid stamp duty in excess of €25 million. The only way we could achieve that was to sell them the site now for as low a price as possible, and sign a separate development agreement. That would cover the costs of the development works and would also give us a large profit. Stamp duty would be payable only on the initial site payment.

Anglo Private occupied the top floor of 1 Burlington Road, an office building developed by Treasury Holdings. I was very familiar with the building because that was also where Bank of Ireland Private was based, and where I regularly came to be lectured regarding overdraft limits and the like by the men in suits.

I caused consternation when I arrived at the building because I wanted to walk up the stairs to the top floor. I think I was the first person ever to do this, and when I reached the top it took Peter's assistant five minutes to find the codes to let me through the stairwell door. 'You can get the lift next time, Mr Kelly,' she told me.

'I like the stairs. They're good for my health,' I replied.

She led me through to the waiting area outside Peter's office. It was a far cry from the 1960s building where I usually borrowed my money. The furnishings were plush and very modern, and it was clear that there were no budget constraints at this end of the bank. Private banking was new to the Irish market, though really it was just posh. There was nothing private about it in the Swiss sense, and we assumed Anglo Private leaked like a sieve, the same as any other bank.

Peter came out of his office and gave me a very warm welcome. 'Hi, Simon, welcome to our humble abode,' he said.

'Thanks, Peter. It's really nice – a far cry from Stephen's Green.'

'You must come up and do some business,' he said. 'We'd love to have you.'

'Stephen's Green is like a private bank to me so I don't need you, Peter,' I answered, knowing this would irk him a little. Peter used to be head of banking in Anglo and his move to the private bank was initially seen as a demotion. But Peter had put his mark on it, and it was now trading as a separate bank from Anglo. The new offices on Burlington Road had been Peter's final drive for independence. He was building the private bank into a bank for Ireland's millionaires. He wanted it to do more than just lend money. Anglo Private would be more like a US investment bank, brokering deals and originating ideas for clients. With the power of the bank's balance sheet behind the deals, it was easy to sell them down. A deal broker who can also provide finance is a powerful and dangerous combination.

As I walked into Peter's corner office it suddenly became very easy for me to understand why he wanted to buy our Burlington Road site: his whole view was dominated by the site. Every day, I imagined, he was looking at it out of his window wondering if he could ever own it.

'I can see why you approached Paddy,' I said to Peter, staring out of his window.

'It's the best building in Dublin,' Peter replied.

'That it is,' I answered.

'And I want to buy it off you,' he said. Peter knew that the best way to approach us was to come straight for us. It was great to skip the usual ritual of trying to work out what the other side wanted.

I got out my laptop and began to walk him through the numbers for the building. We had achieved planning permission for a large high-end office scheme. The site was currently a very big hole in the ground, which was being excavated to make way for the basement car park. Out of this hole in the ground, our gleaming office building was about to grow.

The perfect time to sell an office building is just as you're breaking the ground on the construction, and we were at that stage. Stamp duty on a finished building is 9 per cent, which makes most sales unviable. Pre-selling a building and minimizing the stamp duty would result in a saving of more than €15 million on the deal.

I had prepared some figures, which assumed that the finished building would be leased by a tenant for a rate of €55 per square foot. The standard yield for a building of that nature at the time was 4 per cent. Those figures meant that every square foot of the building had a value of €1,375. Over the entire building this drove out a capital value of almost €350 million. Those figures were pretty standard for the market at the time and Peter did not have a problem with them. We had no tenant for the building, and the trick with a pre-sale like this was to leave behind a certain amount of cash to cover rent until a real tenant was located. We hoped to get away with two years for this rental guarantee, but Peter was looking for us to provide three. The rent was scheduled to be almost €14 million per annum, so that part of the discussion involved figures between €28 million and €42 million.

All the numbers in the deal were huge, but the number that got me most interested was the bottom line. The development costs were due to come in at about €120 million, and that would leave a surplus for the site costs and profit of almost €200 million, depending on the final rent guarantee figure to be agreed. We would have to split this with AIIM, and we would also have to pay off our bank debt, which currently stood at about €42 million on our half of the site. We were looking to walk away with at least €25 million as our portion of the profits.

It was clear from the very beginning of the meeting that Peter really wanted the site. He was building a select property fund to be promoted and financed by Anglo Irish Bank. He told me he had other great deals to go into the fund, but that Burlington Road would be the trophy office building. He was keen to buy the entire building, but I doubted that AIIM would want to sell their half. Also, Paddy and John Flynn were keen to retain a stake in it. I asked Peter if he'd be interested in buying half of our stake, i.e. a quarter of the building.

'Why don't you sell your entire stake, and then come back in on the fund?' he suggested. This was a nice idea in theory, but it was inefficient from a taxation point of view. We would have to pay 20 per cent capital gains tax on our profits from the deal, and there was little point in crystallizing a taxable profit only to reinvest the net proceeds in a property fund. That was our problem.

Peter's problem, as he explained to me, was that he needed the control that would come with ownership of at least 50 per cent. He was happy to own our 50 per cent, and partner with AIIM on the building, but he was not happy to have us as a small residual partner. Buildings with a number of owners are managed by a legal document called a co-ownership agreement, which regulates how decisions are made and how disputes are to be resolved. The majority generally rules, so Anglo would not be happy to own less than 50 per cent.

We agreed to get both sets of agents together to see if a deal could be thrashed out on the commercial terms. I went back to the office very excited about the sale and committed to convincing Paddy and John to sell out, pay the tax and move on. This was our chance to liquidate a large building and release a big lump of cash.

As Paddy and John stewed over the idea, I discussed it with Joe McWilliams in Anglo Irish Bank. Joe had been assigned to us as our main lender, and we understood that his brief was to slow down the juggernaut we had become, and deliver a soft landing.

I was hoping for a soft landing too, and the Burlington Road sale was part of my plan for it, but I could see that Joe was not comfortable with the idea. Anglo Private might have been part of the same bank, but that did not stop Joe trying to keep the loan to himself. 'We would have to keep the cash surplus for Arena Road,' Joe said. Arena Road and Burlington Road were in the same loan package with Anglo Irish Bank, which gave the bank an element of control over the proceeds from the sales. Joe was trying to hold on to the money against other debts in Anglo. He meant this as a subtle put-off. He did not want us to sell too many prime assets, and Burlington Road was certainly on his prime-asset list.

'Joe, the surplus could pay off Arena Road. We've agreed a deal on that anyway,' I replied. This was new territory for Anglo. I was attempting to sell some buildings and pay them off, and they were still trying to hold loan assets and increase profits. Anglo's loan book was growing at an annual rate of over 50 per cent. To achieve and sustain that growth, clients like me had to keep borrowing more and more money. This was fine in theory, but in practice the quality of the deals was getting worse. The growth was not compatible with prudent lending and cracks were appearing. Selling assets was my solution to this problem, and it should have been part of Anglo's as well, but the mystique of Burlington Road meant that they saw it differently.

John and Paddy came around to the idea of selling our entire stake in the building, but while we analysed the deal and tried to figure out ways of offsetting the capital gains tax, the market began to soften. Initially it was subtle, and it didn't seem serious, but it was enough for the Burlington sale to die a quiet death. There were also issues between AIIM and Anglo that we could not overcome, and the marriage for them on a fifty-fifty basis did not seem feasible. It was a real disappointment to me because I could almost smell the money and the freedom the deal would have generated.

While we were looking at selling our 50 per cent of the deal to Anglo Private, AIB had been courting us regarding the debt for the development. We had bought the first part of the site with finance from Anglo, and AIB were asking us to pay off that loan and go with them. That would have broken our Anglo loyalty rule, so we were slow to engage with them.

Our partners, the Flynns, were providing the management for the project and AIB persisted with them about refinancing the deal. We knew that AIB would charge less than Anglo did, and we also thought it might encourage them to take the lease on the building. AIB were due to be in the market soon for new office space, and a great building in a prime location like this was bound to be on their agenda. We hoped that AIIM owning 50 per cent of the deal, with AIB funding the whole deal, might tip the balance in our favour. With the Anglo sale off the agenda for a while, we pushed ahead on the construction and AIB got ready to pay off the Anglo debt on the site.

After a few weeks, the new loan documents were circulated to everybody for signing. When it was complete we had all signed up with AIB for a €120 million facility to pay off Anglo and construct the office building. As I signed the loan document, I knew it was going to cause some new problems. Anglo had been lukewarm on the idea of our paying back their loan with the proceeds of a sale of Burlington Road to their cousins in Anglo Private; now Anglo were going to lose the loan asset to AIB. They did not take kindly to AIB poaching their deal and their client.

I was at the kitchen table at home in Wicklow when my phone lit up: 'Joe McAnglo', my phone name for Joe McWilliams. I picked up the phone and could tell immediately that this was not a normal call.

'What the hell is going on here, Simon?' Joe said, sounding calm but angry.

'What do you mean?' I asked, knowing full well what he meant.

'Don't bullshit. You're paying us off on Burlington Road,' he said.

'You know it's not me, Joe. It's just the way it is,' I said.

'This is not right, Simon. That's our deal.'

Deep down I knew he was right. I was always happy to pay the Anglo premium and leave deals with them because they had always been good to me. I felt that selling was a more acceptable way to pay them off than refinancing with other banks. They would understand us selling buildings, but I knew they would view refinancing as an act of treason.

'Joe, you know it's not me. What can I say?'

'John Flynn Junior didn't even answer my call,' Joe said. 'Do you know that? He can piss off the next time he needs my help, that's for sure.'

I had never heard a banker so annoyed before, and I was

interested in the implications. Lose money or make a mistake on a deal, and a banker might get a little irked. Pay them off – even at a time when they were trying to cool things down – and they would go bonkers.

At that stage my €50-million plan was looking pretty unlikely. The Arena Road sale was agreed but the deal seemed to be going nowhere, and Burlington Road was off the agenda. The sale of the Cablelink building had failed and the other sites had had a few tyre-kickers but no real firm offers.

I picked up the phone and called James Meagher of HT Meagher O'Reilly. 'What's going on with Arena Road?' I asked. When a deal moves as slowly as Arena Road was moving, you know it's on the edge. I needed to try to get the sale back on track with some gentle encouragement and a little bit of stick.

'Banking has become more difficult and this is tied up with another bigger deal,' he said.

He was right about the banking, but this still sounded like bullshit to me. I knew about the bigger deal – the part sale by the Alkens of their site in Sandyford to BOSI – through a back channel, and I also knew it shouldn't be delaying our sale. 'We want to sell it, James. I'll give them a million euro off the price and three months to close if they sign the contract this week,' I said, trying to hand him something to work with.

'That sounds more than fair,' James said. 'I'll call them and get back to you.' He would only get paid if the deal went through, so he had the same incentive as I had.

He called back later that day and the deal was back on. The €1 million discount together with the extra time was enough to get the Alkens over the line. At last I had a contracted sale, and some cash on the way.

By the middle of 2007, cash was becoming a real problem. The steady stream of equity releases from the banks was drying up as the effects of the American sub-prime crisis spread and the banking market got tighter. I was looking at trying to sell assets from our small pool of non-core residential sites. We had shares in land in Killiney and on Fosters Avenue, which should have been attractive to home builders. The problem was that our partners did not want to sell. I put Killiney on the market for €4.5 million through Hamilton Osborne King, and almost had a deal agreed at that level, only to have the site pulled from the market by my partners. They were happy to sell it in theory, but as the reality dawned on them, they lost their nerve. They agreed to try to find a buyer to buy me out of my portion of the deal.

A similar fate befell the Fosters Avenue sale. Two buyers were bidding to pay up to €13.5 million, which was a great price. But, again, the partners in the deal did not want to sell. They felt that a trip back to the planners would add more value.

I was frustrated by this way of thinking. Every grant of planning permission seemed to lead to a new application in an effort to maximize the value. People seemed to overlook the fact that the heat of the market was driving prices up, not gold-plated planning permissions. It was becoming clear to me that it would not be possible to sell any meaningful quantum of assets out of the partnership structures. The final failure of the partnership model became very clear with our office building at Harcourt Street.

In the early 2000s we had purchased the old children's hospital on Harcourt Street for redevelopment. We converted and expanded the Georgian buildings into a large office block, which we leased to BCM Hanby Wallace for over €2.2 million per annum. They were great tenants and the building was in a very good location, so the deal had been a definite success up to that point. We had geared up on the deal a few times and the debt stood at about €36 million.

In late 2007 Adrian Truick rang us with the news that he had had an offer on the building for €65 million from Treasury Holdings. This was almost €30 million more than the bank debt, and it certainly got my attention. 'Take it,' was my immediate answer.

But we only owned 20 per cent of the building so my view was not the only one that counted. A long dialogue of emails was circulated, analysing the offer and the angles with the building. Our partners were very concerned about angles that Treasury might have for the building. Everybody was afraid of doing Treasury a favour, while I just wanted to sell the building and get the money into the bank.

'How are they planning to make money on the deal?' was one partner's question.

'It doesn't matter. Let's just take the price and move on,' was my answer. Treasury owned the KPMG complex next door, so I presumed they wanted to buy our building to expand the site. I was happy to let them have it, but the partners were not so sure and the discussions continued.

After weeks of procrastination, the partnership went back to Adrian looking for €70 million. That would be a yield of 3.14 per cent, which was clearly very rich. Again, the tax and stamp duty costs dominated the email discussions. My view was that capital gains tax was a good problem to have, but the general view was that it was to be avoided at all costs.

After weeks of non-action, we finally agreed to accept Treasury's offer of €65 million. The message back to us from Adrian was short and sweet: 'The offer is gone.' It was as simple as that. We were too late.

The market was continuing to soften and Treasury had clearly recognized this. I was fuming at the manner in which we had blown that deal. If we never sold anything, we were going to end up with a lot of debt and no cash. The partnership model, which had served us so well in the early years of the boom, had become an albatross around our necks. Diverse groups of people did not seem capable of making decisions when it came to selling buildings and taking some money off the table.

It also became clear to me that, despite the softening in the market, most people in the business did not want to sell anything. They all wanted to own more and more.

We had got a very early start in building and owning a large commercial property portfolio. We had also built a large hotel portfolio to shelter the taxable income from those office blocks. This structure permitted us to retain the gross rents and pay minimal taxation. Growing a portfolio with gross rent and no taxation allows for aggressive expansion, and that was the dynamic that had delivered us to this point. We had a prime portfolio of assets but no way of selling them without a very large row. I felt like I was spinning my wheels. No one could leave the arena, it seemed, and I had to resign myself to staying where I was, in hock to Anglo with the exit in sight but out of my reach. To make matters worse, the light on the exit sign was fading as the market weakened.

In the course of my €50-million exit plan, I had successfully sold a number of assets that were solely in my name, and on which decisions were easy to make. To get those sales completed and over the line, I had had to compromise a number of times on price but I always got the sale closed. If I had agreed a deal at €400,000 for an apartment, I was happy to give a €10,000 discount to get the sale over the line and the money in the bank. That is what it takes to get property sold. By the end of 2007, I did not own any investment property, a reflection on what could have been achieved in the rest of our business if we'd structured it differently, or if our partners had shared my desire to realize the value of assets and reduce debt.

The sale of Choice Hotels in the latter half of the year for

€40 million (€12 million for our portion) delivered the cash to make the year a reasonable success, but our development projects were quickly absorbing all the funds I could raise from other parts of the business. I could feel my options getting tighter all through the year as the ways to generate cash flow became fewer.

I lined up three further sales to take us through the run-in to Christmas 2007. I had contracted to sell out my interest in a site in Kilkenny to RQB, and that was to deliver around €2 million. The Arena Road sale was finally due to reach completion and generate €4.5 million. And, as the icing on the cake, Arnotts had agreed to purchase our 20 per cent stake in the Independent Newspapers building. That sale was due to realize at least €3 million.

Together, those three sales should have generated more than €10 million in cash to take the business through December and into a relatively comfortable 2008. All three were lined up for completion in early December, and they looked to be on track. The finance for the Arnotts and RQB deals was being provided by Anglo, so I felt confident that they would both happen. The Arena Road deal had dragged on all year, but the Alkens were now contracted and had paid a large deposit so I wasn't worried about that one drifting into January.

In the end, none of the deals got over the line in time for Christmas 2007, and the Arena Road sale took until April 2008 to complete. Things were about to take a turn for the worse in the market.

8. Teetering

It was a cold, wet February day when I landed at Dublin airport after a month in India with my wife and children. The trip had been a window on to a new world. Back at home in Ireland, everything seemed to be the same, but a new reality had taken hold deep down where we dare not look. We were entering a new era.

During our month away I had not read one newspaper or opened one email or taken one phone call. I had travelled to India to see the real world, and to get away from the false one that Ireland had become. Inside, I had hoped that something would change while I was away. I hoped that maybe I would not be missed, and that things would be better without me.

While I was away, the markets seemed to have completely lost confidence. The trouble had started the previous September, with the run on Northern Rock, and things were only getting worse. As confidence leaked away from the property market, and the banks tightened up on lending, some deals were badly delayed and others fell apart. The slowdown in transaction activity created a serious cash-flow problem for our business. We had traded on a very fine margin for as long as I could remember, and now it looked as if we were running out of road. We needed a continual flow of sales and equity releases to be able to progress the property-development projects and keep the business afloat. This flow of cash had now ceased.

Large property developers were similar to banks in that they borrow short-term money to invest in long-term assets.

A typical property-development project would take seven to ten years to complete. To finance those deals developers often took one- and two-year loan facilities with on-demand clauses. That meant that the banks could call in the loans whenever they wished. Once a loan was called in on a developer, other banks would likely follow, causing the developer's business to collapse. In the same way that Northern Rock was at risk of a bank run, a property developer was also at risk of a bank run. This was not something anyone worried about very much during the good times, but by early 2008, the lenders were spooked, and developers had cause to be nervous. In general, though, the banks were hoping to get through by getting their clients through. They knew that calling in loans and starting runs on developers would bring the whole market tumbling down and cause havoc on their balance sheets.

Developers generally go bust because they do one deal too many or stay in the game too long. I had seen the endgame of the 1980s UK property crash with Paddy and that was still fresh in my mind. I can vividly remember being at meetings with Paddy and his partners in the late 1980s prior to the crash. At those meetings everybody was aware that prices were too high, but they all believed we would have a soft landing: the UK was too strong an economy to have a crash. The situation in Ireland looked familiar. Irish property prices were way too high and we were about to be found out.

I used to discuss the UK crash with bankers and they always thought that Ireland would play out differently. In the UK, when the music stopped, the banks did a complete U-turn on the market and began to dump property assets. That caused the property crash to worsen, which in turn caused more asset dumping. Bank lending governs the price of property, and the Irish bankers were aware of this. The theory went that Irish banks would work through any problems they had, rather than dump the property. We thought we would be smarter than the British, and deal with the problems in a controlled way.

'Welcome back. Are you ready for the fight?' Paddy said, when I walked into the office for the first time in 2008. Dublin seemed surreal after the noise and bustle of India's cities. It was dull and grey, and there was an eerie silence, as if nobody wanted to say what we were all thinking.

'Yes. I'm ready for the fight,' was my answer to Paddy's question. Dealing with a battle is much easier when you recognize that it's coming. A lot of people did not realize there was a battle to be fought, but we were already getting ready and making plans.

While I had been away, the three deals we had lined up before the end of the year had not completed and the cash had run dry. Only the support of our bankers and a lot of luck could keep us solvent. Paddy and Chris had paid a visit to Joe McWilliams in Anglo. At this meeting they had presented the bank with a cash-flow plan. We needed money and Anglo seemed to be the only option. Joe agreed to provide the support we needed. All those breakfasts in the Shelbourne now stood for something, as did the loyalty we had shown to the bank over the years. This was by no means our first visit to Anglo for urgent cash – I had done it many times over the years. The difference this time was that our fundamental position was weak and getting weaker. Normally, for a bank to lend money you needed to give them positive news about the future, but we couldn't find any and neither could the bank. We were bound together because of the debt. If Anglo gave up on us now, they'd have to write off a large percentage of what we owed them, and they didn't want to do that. Giving up on us would also beg bigger questions, because our weakness was a reflection of the weakness of the whole market, although most people did not see it like that yet. With all these factors in play we had little choice but to work together to find a solution.

Anglo's support was by no means unconditional; neither was it open-ended. We agreed to put in place a plan that would allow the bank to extend our equity account to cover our cash needs – a bridging loan while we disposed of certain trophy properties. My €50-million disposal plan had now become everybody's plan. A second condition of Anglo's support was the involvement of Tony Carey from Cooney Carey accountants, who specialized in insolvency; they were retained to co-ordinate and verify the plan. Their other job was to keep me interested and involved in the process. Most of the business was contained in my head, and the bank needed me to help them understand it. I was happy to have the bank need me, but I was very tired of needing the bank.

Soon after my return, I got a call from Joe McWilliams. We arranged to meet the following day at the Shelbourne.

I slept well on the night before the meeting. Calmness and serenity had settled because the truth was out. I needed Anglo and they needed me. We had a chance to be truly honest with each other and to see through the illusion.

I dressed casually on the morning of the meeting and drove up to Dublin. I got to the Shelbourne fifteen minutes early and settled into my seat with a copy of the *Irish Times* and a cappuccino. The room had once been the No. 27 restaurant where I had met Kieran Duggan so many times and arranged some of the loans that had got us into this position. This trouble. The room where I sat waiting to meet with Anglo again had been converted into a bar. The plush carpet had been ripped out and replaced with over-polished floorboards. The simply painted walls had been decorated with vulgar

murals of scenes from Dublin. The boom had removed whatever class and mystique Dublin had had, and the treatment
of the Shelbourne was no different.

Joe was a few minutes late. That was normally my job but
our roles were now reversed as the burden of the portfolio
passed from me to him.

In the property industry, we all knew the story of a famous
meeting that allegedly took place between the house builders
McInerney and Bank of Ireland. I never found out if it was
true, but I liked its message. Developers told it to themselves
when they felt vulnerable and needed to be strong against
the bank. It goes like this. McInerney had a large amount of
debt from Bank of Ireland, and were struggling to repay it.
The bank called the company to a meeting to discuss the debt
and tried to put the squeeze on.

'You owe us a hundred million. What do you propose to
do about it?' said the Bank of Ireland loan manager.

'We intend to keep going as before and work through the
deals,' replied McInerney.

The bank officials appeared to be confused by this answer
so they pressed on. 'Well, we think you're having trouble
with the loan, and we think that this is a problem,' said the
bank, trying to clarify the point.

'Oh! It's a problem, all right, and we can't pay back all the
money, but it's not our problem. It's your problem,' replied
McInerney.

We owed Anglo about €500 million, so by any measure
you may choose, the bank had a problem. We told ourselves
this story to help us sleep at night. I think a lot of people
were telling themselves this story, and others like it.

Joe seemed calm and I sensed he wanted to put me at ease.
'Welcome back,' he said. 'You're looking relaxed.' He was
right. Dealing with a cash-flow problem was as nothing when

compared to what I had seen in India. Also, my values were now different from those of the bank. They valued money, interest and profit – and I was interested in those things, of course, but I valued life, time and happiness even more. My mixed feelings – hoping to keep the business alive, but wanting to step back and live differently – mirrored the kind of feelings I'd had around every major change in my life. The approaching change caused stress, which was then released by the reality of the change. When faced with the facts, however unpleasant they might be, I felt a sense of calm.

I told Joe that Paddy had briefed me on the bank's new support plan.

'We're Anglo clients so we have nowhere else to go,' I said, stating the obvious.

'I want you to focus on ways to get the sales done,' Joe said. 'You need to be creative and find ways to get the money flowing. You're good at that, and that's all I need you to do.' Joe had worked out a long time ago that I did not feel any emotion for the assets. I had no secret agendas on properties and there was nothing in our portfolio that I would not be happy to sell.

'No problem, Joe. I'd sell it all if I could. You know that.'

'You have also got to find a way of sorting out the partners. We will fund them to buy assets from you, if need be. We need to get them focused on the sales as well.' This was the crucial point. In most cases, the only way to deliver sales was to do deals with our partners. Easy finance from Anglo would certainly grease the wheels in that process.

That turned out to be our last meeting at the Shelbourne. We were now in battle mode, and our rearguard action would be carried out henceforth in businesslike meetings at Anglo's offices or at 128 Baggot Street. The market was unravelling and the frills were disappearing. Credit was getting tighter while my calmness was growing deeper. I was glad that the truth was finally being recognized.

The next day, at Joe's suggestion, I met Tony Carey at Cooney Carey's offices in Sandyford. I drove out, not knowing what to expect from him. Joe had reassured me that I would get on well with him, and that they had chosen him for this reason and for his steady hand. I parked my car on the street beside his building and made my way up to the office in the lift. It was a cheap lift, the same sort that we had put into so many buildings. I hate cheap lifts and they seemed to be everywhere. I rattled my way slowly up to the third floor.

The receptionist escorted me along the corridor towards Tony's office. There was a games room on the right-hand side. It looked as if it had never been used. The TV and Sony PlayStation sat idly, shining as they had on the day they were unwrapped. It looked and felt like a modern company headquarters, but something seemed wrong. It was as if everybody had been told to be happy. The smiles looked fake. I knew I was the victim and they were the predators. I could sense them whispering, 'There he is — that's the guy who owes Anglo all that money!'

These early meetings were like the discussions a surgeon has with his patient prior to an operation. The purpose of the chat is to prepare the patient for the procedure. Talking it out helps the patient or client to deal with the consequences, be they good or bad. We can all accept bad news once we've had time to get used to it, and nobody ever wants to be shocked. 'What is unacceptable today becomes acceptable tomorrow' was one of Paddy's favourite sayings.

After the opening pleasantries, Tony got to the point. 'I love the way you do business,' he said. 'You're not to change that.' He was referring, I assumed, to the informal way in

which we carried out our deals. Handshakes and verbal agreements were the basis of our business. The lawyers were always
in the background but we never let them dictate the agenda.
We valued trust. If we couldn't trust you, we didn't want to
do business with you.

Otherwise, Tony's message was that he thought we had
great assets; that we were going to get through this; and that
he wanted to make sure I was happy and engaged with the
process. I left the meeting ready to press the plan into action
to the best of my ability.

The plan itself was cumbersome but enlightening. We were
going to go through every line of our statement of affairs
with a fine-tooth comb. We would look at every asset and
debt in detail and all assumptions were verified from source
documentation. It would amount to a twenty-year audit of
our affairs by Tony Carey on behalf of Anglo.

Gillian from my office became central to the plan. She had
a fantastic ability to map out the numbers, unburdened by
any emotion about the business or our plight. We developed
a very large spreadsheet listing every asset and its cash flow.
The names by which we knew the deals were replaced with
numbers ranging from 1 to 178. Number 1 was my family
home in Wicklow and number 178 was an apartment at
Canary Wharf in London that I owned. In between were the
projects that made up a life's work. Burlington Road was
number 66 and Harcourt Street was number 13. Those should
have been two easy sales, I thought, but the ball had been
dropped.

All through March and April we verified the base data for
the plan and made projections for cash flow and capital
expenditure. When all the data was submitted to paper, it
looked so neat and organized. The turmoil, excitement and
energy that had been expended in acquiring and developing

those assets were now boiled down to a few figures. This was how it had begun for me: reduce the project to a series of numbers that you can manage on your computer. The numbers changed over the years but the approach was the same. When the numbers are submitted to a spreadsheet model on a computer screen they provoke no offence. The computer does not wince at a minus or negative number. Once there is a number, the machine is happy.

The plan called for us to sell about fifteen assets, and the surplus from those assets was to fix everything. In other words, it was another version of my €50-million plan. In 2007 I had failed in my plan because our partners didn't want to sell. In 2008 my challenge was to find a way of selling when everybody else wanted to do the same thing and nobody wanted to buy. It was clear from the very beginning that we were not the only clients working with Anglo on a liquidity plan. In April 2008 the sale of Arena Road finally completed – more than twelve months after I had agreed the deal. Our surplus was over €4 million, as planned, and that eased the cash-flow pressure in the short term. We would not be going back to the bank for any further funding until the formal loan offer was signed off, approving the extended equity loan. It looked as if we would need to increase it from €30 million to more than €100 million, with planned sales bringing it back down to €70 million by the end of 2008.

By the end of April we were ready with the numbers, and new systems were in place. Tony Carey had issued a glowing report to the bank about our business and our understanding of the challenge ahead. By this time we knew that the bank had its own liquidity issues. Deborah Rae, who was my day-to-day contact at Anglo managing the plan, had made this clear to me. As our plan progressed, it became clear that the bank was working on a much bigger plan to try to ensure its own survival.

With the figures in place and the targets set in stone, Paddy and I decided to meet the senior people in Anglo to express our gratitude. A little tour of the bank was always useful and we wanted to show that we were alive, well and dealing with the issues.

Walking with Paddy to Anglo was never simple. Invariably he would know most of the people on the street and we would stop and say hello to everybody. We bounced up the road with confident, happy faces but every person we met looked pressured and worried.

'How is it going?' Paddy would say, as we bumped into somebody we knew.

'Badly. What's happened?' was always the answer. Everybody in the property business was feeling the squeeze. Things were slowly grinding to a halt.

When we got to the bank, we announced ourselves at Reception. The girls on the desk must have seen me a million times, but I always told them who I was and who I was seeing.

'Simon and Paddy here to see David Drumm,' I said, as I approached the desk. Seeing David was always nice and I didn't mind if my bankers knew that I could see him whenever I needed to. The CEO of a bank keeps away from most of the lending decisions, but it was still useful to be spotted in the bank with the top management.

I have been to every part of the Anglo building on St Stephen's Green over the years, but this was my first time in the corner office of the CEO. David's office was a little more spacious than the normal manager's quarters, but it was functional in line with the whole bank. He had a small boardroom table and I took a seat at this with Paddy while David finished a phone call. He quickly wrapped it up and came over to take a seat with us.

'What's going on? It's crazy,' he said. The freeze was on in the property market, and bank shares had plummeted. Anglo's shares, which had peaked at more than €17, had recently been as low as €6. The graph was only pointing in one direction.

'Bloody hedge funds are targeting us,' David added, clearly annoyed. 'I'll show them when I announce the results.' The bank was about to report and I think he hoped that the short sellers would be squeezed.

'We're just here to say thanks for the support,' Paddy said, turning the discussion towards our problem. 'We'll do everything we can to fix our little problem and get back on track,' he added. Like David, Paddy still believed that we could beat this rap and that the country could regain its upward trend. I stayed quiet on that. I didn't have his confidence. I had worked out the numbers, and I was also an observer of asset prices around the world. While our debts were rising, our asset values were crashing and liquidity was gone. I knew how the story was going to end. I had to play the game for Paddy's benefit and for the bank's. Deep down I was thinking about lifeboats and making sure I had one.

The tone of the meeting with David stayed optimistic, and we all joked about the old days. I think we secretly yearned for the good parts of the old days to return. We knew that bad things were going on outside the walls of the bank. Talking about the old days was a useful way of ignoring those events, even for a few minutes.

We left David and walked down the corridor. As we passed Sean FitzPatrick's office, we paused and looked in to see if he was free. He beckoned us. 'Hiya, lads, how's it going?' he said, in a happy, upbeat voice. His office was much smaller than David's and was strewn with documents. It was like a private headquarters from which he ran his own business affairs: the job of chairman at Anglo was not all-consuming for him and he was now involved in a number of other businesses around the world. When David Drumm had got the top job as CEO, Sean, stepping up to chairman, was conscious of the need to let David run the show, and the other investments seemed to be keeping Sean busy.

'Great, Sean. We were just in with David, saying hello and discussing things,' Paddy replied.

'Strange times, Paddy. Anyway, we'll all get through them,' Sean replied. Then, turning to me, he said, 'You should have a look at my oil-well deal, Simon. It would interest you.' The bank knew I was very interested in non-property deals, and I was glad that this had gone all the way to the top.

'You're in the right business there, Sean,' I said. Oil was more than $150 a barrel at the time.

'You should have a look at buying into the deal,' Sean added. Even now, we were talking about new deals – new deals had always been the solution to old deals. A new deal with new profits could fix everything. Sean certainly seemed to have a lot of confidence about his oil field in Nigeria.

That one-hour tour of the bank's top management reminded me of why I was an Anglo client. Anglo would stand by you and help you when you needed help. Healthy clients meant a healthy bank. That part of the Anglo culture was truly unique, and that day I certainly appreciated it.

As Paddy and I walked down the stairs and out into the street, I felt warmth for the place. It was as though they were a concerned parent putting their arms around us in our time of need. It was as though we would be together for many more years to come.

'That was useful,' Paddy said, as we left the bank. We had been there hundreds of times together but this time had felt different. He was aware that his comment was a major under-statement. 'There is no other bank in the world where you can walk in and meet the CEO and the chairman for a chat like that.'

Walking away down the street that day, I was proud and glad to be a client of Anglo. I had been courted and chased by other banks over the years but I had always resisted. A roll-call of names and relationships flashed through my mind as I remembered all the people I had dealt with in the bank. It was a long list. I had always felt that my relationship with Anglo was one of friendship and support. Their support for the liquidity plan cemented it. I also had a sense of guilt about the areas in which I had let them down. When we lost money, I felt guilty.

As our private business was just about surviving, thanks to the Anglo lifeline, RQB was beginning to fall apart. It was starved of cash. We had managed to complete on the London Unex deal at the end of 2007, but that was the last time RQB was able to raise cash from any investor for any project. In completing the purchase of Unex, RQB had used all its spare cash and overdraft facilities. The existing RQB projects had ring-fenced cash reserves to carry them through the two or three years of the planning process but they were dwindling as the months passed and interest and other costs were paid. As the cash ran out, and with no further cash being raised, Bank of Ireland and AIB appointed receivers to each asset. With the value of land collapsing all around us, there was no incentive for the investors to raise new cash, and the banks were unwilling to write down the debt amounts if new equity was invested.

(RQB was finally put into liquidation in 2009. All of its sites had received significant equity investments, but even this could not withstand the crash in values. At the time of writing, none of the RQB assets has been sold or progressed in any way by the banks and their receivers. They are now part of the oversupply of land that exists all over the Dublin market.)

Being popular with Anglo did not mean that delivering our plan would be easy. The final Cooney Carey report was sent to the bank and circulated among the decision-makers on the credit committee. We arranged a final meeting to present our case and to seal the deal. It was now May and the crisis was intensifying all the time. Tony met with me on the morning of the meeting and told me what the bank were thinking and what they wanted to hear. The meeting, I thought, would be like breaking bad news to a close friend. We approached it with complete honesty and transparency because they were the only weapons we had left. Miracles do not happen in this business. We could not and did not want to hide from the facts.

David Kelly and I sat down to work on our PowerPoint presentation. It was full of simple numbers, and the core message was clear: we were good clients with great invest-ment property assets. We needed support through this credit crunch to complete certain developments. The profits from those projects would, over time, provide the cash flow to fix the balance-sheet hole. In the interim, we needed to borrow more money to keep solvent while we undertook an asset-sale programme. The profits from the property-development assets would provide the cash to de-leverage the balance sheet in the long term. Basically, it was a cash squeeze but one that we could survive due to the quality of our assets. Our plan was really an Anglo plan designed to keep a key client afloat. The bank could not afford for people to see weakness in its clients or its overall loan book.

We had arranged for the meeting to take place in the main boardroom of the bank. We needed that room because of the number of people who were attending the presentation and to reflect the seriousness of the situation. Paddy Kelly, Chris Kelly, David Kelly, Gillian and I were there from our office, with Tony Carey and a full team from Anglo, including Pat Whelan, who was head of banking.

I went through the slides, explaining where we were and why we had a problem. The key pressure for us at this point was to arrange the capital to complete certain projects. The cash could only come from Anglo because the assets that we were working on were already financed by the bank. Our overall interest balance was also out of line but this was mainly due to non-performing assets, like Carton Golf Club, and the running interest cost on our equity loan. The majority of our assets were income-producing and generating a surplus of rent over their interest costs. Our business could be split into two halves. The profitable investment property was generating surplus cash flow, and the negative cash-eating property development needed support. The numbers were all big, but we could make it – or so we hoped.

Prior to starting the liquidity plan, Anglo had been concerned about our potential exposure to other banks. They had presumed we had built up large debt positions with other banks. At an early stage in the plan they realized that this was not so, which provided them with a degree of comfort. The majority of our other bank debts were on smaller investment-property loans and we had little or no development exposure with them. That meant Anglo did not have to worry too much about a rogue bank squeezing our business. Anglo had provided 73 per cent of our overall debts. I wished that it were closer to 100 per cent. I could feel the other banks beginning to panic and I could see the squeeze coming down the road in the near future.

'It's a great plan,' Pat Whelan said. 'But who is going to make sure it happens?'

'I will, Pat. I'll sell the assets,' I said. That was the answer Pat had wanted to hear. He thought that Paddy would not fully support the plan because it involved selling crown-jewel assets. He needed to hear that we were committed to cutting down on the assets and moving forward. I was telling the complete truth when I told him this, and it was easy for him to believe me. By now the whole bank knew that from 2005 I had tried to move away from property and into trading businesses, so they could accept that I would sell the property assets.

We wrapped up the meeting and I knew we had the money. I had a fair idea that this was the case even before the meeting. If they did not lend us the money, large chunks of their loan book would move into default and that was not what they wanted at this sensitive time. Their share price was continuing to plummet.

As we walked back to the office after the meeting, Tony called. 'Well done, Simon,' he said. 'You did really well in there. They're with you.' We were approved to borrow up to €100 million to tide us over until 2009. The funds would allow us to complete the various projects, and pay all deficit interest costs for 2008. They also provided money for office costs and salaries. Everything would be covered, allowing me to focus on trying to raise some cash and sell some assets.

A simple set of loan-offer documents arrived soon after the meeting, and we signed them, putting the loan formally in place. Almost immediately, the money began to flow.

For the first few months, the plan was a pleasure to operate. We had loads of money and we paid every bill on time.

Our partners began to smell a rat. We had never been so efficient in the past, and now we were paying interest on the day it was due.

'You've never been so fast at making payments,' Brian McCormack said to me, after one of our partnership meetings. Every quarter we'd all had to write a cheque to make up for the interest shortfall on the Carton House Hotel. It had €68 million of debt on it and the business wasn't generating even half the annual interest bill. In the past, this money was always very difficult to find, and I had always been late. We were now making the payments on the day the interest was due. I could see the envy in our partners' eyes as they struggled to find the cash. They were now the ones making payments late.

I told Brian about our new facility with Anglo. I was very proud of it, and we were completely open with everybody about how we were being funded. I began to get some probing questions from other developers about how they should go about getting a similar facility. It was clear from my meetings with them that we had plenty of company in the insolvency club. The difference was that not everybody had the support of Anglo. I noticed that at first other developers seemed to feel sorry for us, requiring this loan facility, but then, as time passed and things got worse, they started to feel jealous.

Through the summer, we implemented the plan in accordance with the agreement. We closed off a few more small sales, which built up further goodwill within the bank. But even as we got more comfortable with the plan, the property market and the banking crisis continued to worsen. When we started the process with Anglo, Bear Stearns was being rescued by JPMorgan Chase with the support of the US government. That was like the canary in the mine. After the demise of Bear, the markets went very quiet. A number of second-tier banks and mortgage companies were wound up, and eventually liquidity became non-existent.

In spite of the problems in the wider market, we stuck to the plan. We did not spend a penny that was not provided for. I had toured the other banks after signing up the Anglo deal to explain to them the programme we were undertaking. In each one, I heard new tales of woe. Everything was frozen and the market was spiralling down. Everybody was chasing interest payments so they could say that their loans were not in default, but there did not seem to be any real answers.

I saw this at first hand on a deal I had with AIB to refurbish and extend the old Bewley's premises on Westmoreland Street. AIB had provided me with €20 million of development finance, but the deal was on the ropes because we did not have enough rental income to pay the annual interest. The rental income was agreed and very close to being available, but we needed to invest a further €500,000 in the building to secure the tenants. That would have saved the whole €20 million of debt because the interest could have been funded. The deal went back and forth for months, and all the bank was concerned about was the interest: they were desperate to find a way to show the interest was being paid so that the loan could remain in the 'performing' column. They promised to finance the project further once a payment of €250,000 had been made. They were willing to promise almost anything just to be able to show that the €20 million loan was being serviced. In the end, we couldn't make the €250,000 interest payment because it was not an approved item as per the plan. That forced the loan into default and AIB into convulsions. The €20 million loan was non-recourse, which meant I was not subject to a personal guarantee for the sum owing. In the end I was able to walk away from it. A different approach from the bank would certainly have saved that loan. Banks were clearly becoming irrational, making decisions based on very short-term horizons.

We had retained HT Meagher O'Reilly to try to sell property assets for us. We issued them with the asset list on a confidential basis, and arranged to meet in Anglo after they had reviewed the sites and researched any potential sales.

I met up with Declan O'Reilly and Adrian Truick from HT, and we walked up to Anglo together to deliver the report. Declan and Adrian had years of experience in commercial property as agents and advisers. They knew what was going on and what might be possible in that market. It was not looking like good news: there was not much of a market left even to discuss.

'What do they want to hear, Simon? Nothing's selling,' Declan said, as we approached the bank. It was a beautiful summer day, but the warm air could do nothing about the frozen property market. All of the banks had ceased to finance new property deals, and existing deals were on limited life support. Putting up properties officially for sale just wasted money on advertising. There were no buyers because there was no finance. Everybody cannot leave the market and sell up at the same time, because if they do, there will be no market. This was what had happened in Dublin.

This deep-freeze phase had a false air. I knew that property prices would collapse once a big deal or two was done at the true market price. Nobody seemed to want to find out where this true price was, so nothing was being sold. In the 1980s the price for land fell to the level of the equity amount in the deal, which was generally about 20 per cent. With no bank debt, all you can invest is the equity. In good

times, the leverage drives up the price; in a crash, it drives
it down.

'The last big deal to sell in this town was yours on Arena
Road,' Adrian said to me. 'Do the bank not know this?' He
was puzzled by the need for a meeting because he knew there
was little he could do.

'They know it. They just don't want to face it,' I said. 'They
want to hear what you think things might sell for and that
you'll try to sell them. That's all we can do.'

I think we all knew that trying to sell assets was a complete
waste of time, but Anglo wanted us to keep at it. Even so,
they weren't willing or able to facilitate us in every instance.
I had a few deals done to sell minority stakes in Anglo buildings to Anglo clients and the bank had refused to fund them.
That was a clear signal to me that we were not the only problem. We were only a small piece of it. The Arnotts deal was
always 'about' to happen when I asked the bank about it, but
I could tell it was a dead duck. I had a similar experience on
a sale of my 10 per cent stake in the Morrison Hotel. We had
listed it as a done deal in the plan because I had a contract
with Hugh O'Regan, and the bank had told me they would
fund it. All Anglo had to do was to lend €2 million more and
use that to pay off €2 million of the equity facility. In the end
they did not do it. It was becoming clear to me that we might,
if anything, be in better health than the rest of the market.
No client seemed able to borrow any money, even if it was
to pay off Anglo and help the bank. Everybody seemed to be
broke.

The meetings in Anglo were now held in small, stuffy
rooms: the days of the grand boardrooms were over. We
squeezed into a small meeting room to review the sales
progress with HT Meagher O'Reilly. There was despond-
ency in the air as the glum-faced participants took their seats.

There were some new faces on the Anglo side, sitting with Joe McWilliams. I guessed they had been sent in to learn how to deal with their own clients who were in the same position. We seemed to have become a test case.

'Right, guys, where are we at?' was Joe's opening line. His tone was upbeat, but it sounded hollow.

Adrian and Declan told their story of discussions and potential deals, but no actual sales. They did their best to put a positive spin on what might be possible, but it was clear that nothing was. There were not going to be any significant sales. Whenever the bank attacked me on this, which was very rarely, I only had to mention the Arnotts and the Morrison transactions. If the bank were not willing to fund deals like these, what chance did I have?

Despite the state of the market, I had managed to achieve a few small sales. We sold a restaurant on Pembroke Street to the tenant for €1.6 million, and this was a great deal for us. It allowed us to clean up our whole Permanent TSB loan book and generate some cash flow for ourselves. We also managed to sell off a stake in a medical business for almost €1 million, and a few residual houses and apartments. The market was still accepting small sideline deals, but nothing of scale or significant value.

Joe McWilliams and I had regular meetings through the summer of 2008 to review our progress. When he and I were together, we could both admit what we knew: that the market was trashed, and there were going to be a lot of very bad loans, including some of ours. It was a real crash and we were going to be stuck for five or ten years or even longer. It was going to be our Great Depression. The problems in the market did not stop with the developers. The banks themselves were under huge stress.

'There's a quiet run happening on the banks,' I told Paddy.

I could see the money draining from the system every time I met a bank. Every time they said things were fine, I could see through their lies. They wished things were fine but that was a million miles from the truth.

As the life was sucked from the property market, I could see the real economy following quickly behind. We had a large exposure to the hotel business, and it was falling off a cliff. The economy was clogged with toxic loans and they were bringing down the entire system. People had begun to hoard cash.

Summer in Dublin is normally quiet because people go on holiday, and very few deals get done. A lot of faith was being placed on a bounce in the market in September, when people would be back to look at some bargains. That was the market's view but it was never mine. I knew that buyers had not merely gone for the summer.

When the world arrived back from its summer holidays, things got a whole lot worse.

On 7 September, the two monsters of the American mortgage market, Freddie Mac and Fannie Mae, were nationalized. That was a shock, and it made us all look at the banks in Ireland with new eyes. I told anybody with money in the Irish system to move it. Whatever money I had, which was very little, I transferred to a bank overseas.

Lehman Brothers filed for Chapter 11 bankruptcy protection on 15 September, and this caused all money movements to freeze. Irish banks, heavily exposed to property as they were, had been struggling for months to borrow money; now only the European Central Bank would lend to them. By the time the Irish government had guaranteed the liabilities of Anglo and five other Irish banks, any lingering thought of survival had left my mind. I was mentally prepared for the end, and I began to make concrete plans. We were not getting out of this one. Neither was Ireland.

By December, the property business was a very quiet place. An eerie silence had fallen over the whole town as the implications of the world crash settled in. Nobody was socializing and everybody was saving money. This was to be a first taste of a deep recession for most people. All corporate events were cancelled and the only Christmas parties were secret affairs.

We had booked ours in a restaurant in Baggot Street called Chez Max. We had managed to lease the restaurant to its management earlier in the year despite the bad market and we were keen to support them. I knew it would be our last meal together as the team from the office, and I wanted us all to have a good time. As the wine flowed we began to consider the uncertain future.

Paddy asked everyone at the table to predict the share price of Anglo Irish Bank in December 2009, twelve months hence. The bids varied from person to person, ranging from fifty cents to €2.50. I waited until the end to offer my prediction.

'Nil,' I said. 'They won't be around next December.' I poured myself another large glass of red wine.

9. Insolvency

The end of December 2008 was a nightmare. The Anglo plan was in tatters as the bank reneged on agreed payments. I had a queue of suppliers waiting to get paid their final invoices for the redevelopment of Tulfarris Golf Club and Resort and they were getting very nervous. We had agreed to complete the building works there as part of the plan, but the bank was now coming up short.

Vanessa Murphy worked for us as the project manager for the building and refurbishment at Tulfarris and she asked me to join her at a meeting with Anglo two days before Christmas. The bank was refusing to pay out to suppliers and she was pleading with me for help.

I revved up for another meeting in Anglo, hunting for money. We had been given the last meeting slot with the bank on the last day that money could be transferred before Christmas. This was going right down to the wire. I had given everything I could to delivering the plan, so the bank owed me those payments, or so I thought.

Vanessa and I walked across the Green in the cold dark night. I was struggling to get motivated because the vibe from the bank seemed to get worse at every meeting.

A Christmas tree was in place in the Anglo reception area and an effort had been made to capture the festive spirit, but nothing could conceal the atmosphere. It was as if a death had occurred. In a way it had: a few days earlier, Sean Fitz-Patrick had resigned as chairman after it was revealed that for a number of years he had hidden personal loans from the bank on the balance sheet of Irish Nationwide in the run-up to Anglo's annual accounts; and David Drumm had followed him out of the door the next day.

I had spent the previous few weeks with Deborah Rae in the bank preparing an equity plan for 2009. We had done a reasonable job on the 2008 plan, sticking as close to the agreed cash flow as we could, and the cash needed for 2009 was going to be a lot less. The new plan was to pay interest on the Anglo bank loans and to reduce overheads. Building was over, and selling was not an option, so hanging on was the only game we could play. The sales we had achieved in 2008 were in contrast to the rest of the market, which had completely shut down, but we could no longer bank on miracles like those.

Against this background, I entered the bank looking for some money.

I tried to paint a very straight picture for Deborah: 'These are real people who have done this work for the bank. You have to pay them.'

'It's over budget, Simon, and I need Joe to sign it off,' she replied. Joe was not around, which was very convenient. She promised to sit down with him in the morning and try to get a payment off him. She felt for the suppliers, but the bank was the bank. 'Don't shoot me. I'm only the messenger,' she said.

We left the bank as the lights were going out and the cleaners came in. Little did they realize that they were now richer than the bank.

The next day Deborah conveyed Joe's response: 'No.' I rang Joe to get an explanation. I wanted to know why, after all the years of work and sweat, we were going to fall short with these people. Why was it that the honest suppliers in Tulfarris, who had worked and toiled, were going to be the fall guys? Anglo was still getting its interest paid. Why could these people not be paid?

'We can't do it, Simon,' Joe said. 'We don't have the money.'

'If that's the case, Joe, I want you to put in a receiver,' I said. 'Lock the gates and put a big padlock on it for ten years. It's the best thing for that place.' If the bank were not going to fund the hotel, which was now their project, they were going to have to tidy up the mess and deal with the fallout. When we had started the cash-flow plan with Anglo in February, we had set it up to last the full year. To fall short on Christmas Eve, with only seven days in the year left, was a real tragedy.

The receiver was appointed in early January, and the hotel was opened shortly afterwards. The bank took the benefit of the work carried out by the suppliers but it did not pay them. That left a bitter taste in my mouth.

In early January, I sat down in the office and worked out a new plan. We were on our own now because the Anglo plan was not being extended. The capital expenditure was complete on almost all of our outstanding projects, but we would not be able to service our interest costs. From now on it was only a matter of time until we received the fatal blow. Anglo had taken us off life support. How long could we survive without them? Not long, I thought.

The annual running cost for the management of the Redquartz business was about €2 million. That was made up mostly of legal and accountancy fees, the salaries and over-heads for the office team. Left to our own devices we were not going to be able to carry the overhead cost, so my attention now focused on that. We had to cut our costs but manage the same amount of deals. We had brought the team as far as we could but we could not go on.

My brother Chris and I looked at the list of staff and had

to make some tough decisions. We had to cut to the bone. Everybody in the office had to go, bar three. The office also had to go because we would not be able to fund the interest cost on the building. We postponed the news until February, but I think the staff knew something bad was coming, and a depressed air had settled over the team. We were now marking time until the end and everybody knew it. The only question was who would put the knife in first.

Chris and I took our seats in the boardroom on a Monday in February 2009 and, one by one, we called in the staff. The message was the same: we have to make you redundant, and we have to do so now to ensure we can make the redundancy payment. Sending those people off into the great unknown was difficult for me because they were great. Our team in the office would do anything for me. Their loyalty and dedication were never in question. I could see the fear in their eyes: the economy was in freefall and unemployment was rising at a terrifying rate.

Money was tight and we could not add very much to the statutory redundancy package. I would have liked to do more, but I did not have the power. Little did they know where I planned to get the money to pay the redundancy packages. I had decided that Anglo owed it to the team to fund them and I planned to pay them from a rent account with money that was due to the bank under a loan agreement. Those people had given their all through the year to help the bank, and deliver the cash-flow plan, and I was going to make sure the bank made the final payment, whatever the cost. I knew that this would go down like a lead balloon in Anglo, but I also knew it was the right decision. Left on its own, the bank would ignore those people and leave them with no money, as it had the suppliers in Tulfarris.

With the office reduced to three, there were now vast spaces around each desk, and the ghosts of the missing people seemed to haunt the space they had occupied. I never had a desk in the office, and now that I had my choice, I wanted none of them. By this stage RQB and Boundary were gone from 128 Lower Baggot Street, and I began to find reasons not to go into the office.

Anglo asked me to work up a new plan for 2009, based on paying their interest costs and running the projects with the new reduced overhead. They were very clear that when they said 'reduced' they meant almost nil. They were willing to pay a little to have the assets managed, but not enough to retain our few staff.

I addressed my new task as though by remote control: I was now a disinterested third party, observing myself. These were no longer my assets and I was no longer working for myself. I was the bank's drone. I walked their corridors and went to their meetings as a dead man.

'We will pay you to work on the deals,' Joe said, at one of these new death meetings, trying to give me some incentive.

Everything now seemed to be in black and white, like an old movie.

'What about Chris?' I said, and Joe was silent. Chris was sitting beside me when I asked, but Joe had ice in his veins.

'What about Paddy?' I said, and Joe was still silent.

He saw the look in my eye and was forced to answer. 'The bank thinks Paddy is ready for retirement,' he offered, and that was that. Years of loyalty from Paddy were to be forgotten. Loyalty was looking a lot like stupidity.

Why me? I was thinking. Everybody knew I hated the business, and they certainly knew I was not too fond of banks. I had just taken Thomas Read's into examinership with the express plan of getting the courts to cram the bank debt with ACC. I was never shy in expressing my opinion that bank debt would need to be written off.

I remember Joe telling me in a meeting that if I was successful in Thomas Read's it would spell the end of corporate lending in Ireland. I left the room that day wishing for it to happen, and hoping to be the one to make it happen. Screw the system, I thought. The banks need to learn a few lessons.

This new state of mind bothered me. I did not want to be dead. I wanted to be a vibrant giver, not the bank's zombie, walking around the ghost town that Dublin seemed set to become. The price for my soul had been set at €200,000 per annum of which €100,000 was to be a bonus, based on performance. I needed the money and it would have made everything easy. It would have been like injecting heroin into my arm. As all around me collapsed, I could close my eyes and cling to the warm rush of the Anglo money. In the past, they had bought me for millions, and now the offer was two hundred grand – and I needed their money like an addict needs the needle. Cold turkey was frightening to consider.

Bouncing along the N11 in my jeep in March 2009, after thinking about all of these things, I picked up the phone and called Joe. I told him I'd thought about the offer, and that I was going to say no. If he needed a Kelly, my brother would do it, and do a better job at that. He was still pretty fresh and confident about the business. He was a far cry from the cynic I had become. I told Joe I would be there in the background to assist Chris whenever he needed it.

It was as simple as that. I was free. Joe offered no resistance. I could sense he approved of my decision. Deep down, I suspect, he wanted to walk away as well.

A lot had passed between us, but I felt that this was a suitable end. He would stay and I would go. As I sped along the motorway, the whole world opened up to me. I could do anything and be anyone. I put my foot to the floor, and

pumped up the stereo. This was my movie moment and I
bellowed out the tunes at the top of my voice.

In the end it was Hugh McGivern who wielded the knife.
That seemed appropriate. It was better to be struck down by
an honest enemy than a false friend.

We lay down and accepted our fate – fighting would have
made it harder. The game was up and everybody knew it,
but we seemed to be the only people willing to face it. As
we pulled away from court that day in March 2009, I knew
we were at the beginning of a journey that would be long
and complex, but that, in the end, peace would come. Calm
descended upon me. Simon Kelly, the property tycoon,
was dead. 'Long live the new Simon Kelly' was my secret
thought.

After the court announcement on 16 March 2009, Anglo
went into shock. They knew that the cash-flow plan was in
the bin, but they had not thought through the implications.
We had talked with them about a scheme of arrangement,
but I don't think they understood what it meant. They were
listening and nodding approval, but our message was not
getting through. We were on the hospital trolley on the way
out of intensive care. The problem was that we were heading
away from the recovery area and towards the morgue. Anglo
found the truth very difficult to deal with.

'Why did you have to make that statement?' Tony Carey
asked me, reflecting the bank's confusion.

'What's wrong with the truth?' I asked him.

'Anglo now has to work out what to do. You've forced
their hand,' he said.

Anglo was shocked, worried and running scared. It was
clearly not ready for the truth, even though it had encouraged
us towards this action. The world now knew that the emperor

had no clothes, but the people at Anglo still wanted to pretend they wore flowing robes of silk and satin. The nationalized bank that was clearly bankrupt wanted to pretend that their clients were going to make it.

Their reaction seemed strange to us because we had kept them informed all through the process. I suspect that our statement to the court had forced them to take legal advice, and that this advice had stunned them. As bankers, they seemed to have no experience with insolvency. The lawyers were now leading the bank, and this was never a good sign.

In the days after the court announcement, a silence descended on our business. I had to keep checking my telephone to make sure it was on. Nobody was calling, not even the bank. We had used the 'B word', as I liked to call it, and threatened to use the 1988 Bankruptcy Act. That is a simple but effective piece of legislation that struck terror deep into the bank's heart. It was their worst nightmare. They could not deal with a runaway developer who was willing to tell the truth, and who was also willing to follow it up with action. Our use of the word 'bankruptcy' had pushed our relationship with Anglo into a totally new place.

After a few days of silence, I called Joe on his mobile. A week had now passed since our St Patrick's Day appearance in the *Irish Times* following the McGivern judgment. I was working on the details of a scheme of arrangement under the Bankruptcy Act. I could sense that Joe knew this.

'We're checking out our options,' Joe told me. 'You've forced our hand.' I could smell the stench of lawyers down the telephone line. I could almost feel their grubby fingers rifling through our files, and searching for ways to defend by attack. If we chose to take action, the bank had no defence. I knew that because I had been studying the bankruptcy laws for more than twelve months.

'We can only defend ourselves by putting the whole lot into receivership,' Joe said. 'Everybody.'

That summed up the bank's problem. I could not sell any property in the past because of the complex partnership structure we had used. That was also why the bank could not single us out for special treatment. We were a minority shareholder connected to about €3 billion of debt and we could not be isolated. The bank could not put a single person into receivership without putting everybody into the same process. That was a frightening prospect. I had emailed the bank and our partners pointing out this fact – which I had discovered in my study of the Bankruptcy Act – in 2008, but nobody had paid attention to it. Our structure was built for success and tax efficiency, not insolvency. We and our partners were chained to this sinking ship and going down together. I was reading and thinking about these things, but everybody else was pushing forward, hoping for the best.

Joe and I arranged to meet in a few days' time. The bankruptcy list is heard every Monday in the courts and Joe was convinced that we were ready to go into the next. There was real fear in his voice. The bank's problem was now a lot worse than mine.

We sat down to review our options with our advisers. I knew the end was near and I did not want to extend the process by entering into a scheme of arrangement. Paddy felt the same, and we both wanted to keep the wider partnerships exempt from the process.

I had produced a document for Anglo prior to the court case offering to pass over all our assets to the bank, in return for the right to walk away from the liabilities. This plan arose from an honest assessment of the reality of both our situations, and the bank knew it, but they seemed powerless to act. They were still coming to terms with the general meltdown, and I was working too fast for them in offering to walk away.

'I know it's a good idea, Simon, but we're not ready for this yet,' Joe said to me.

'You'd better get ready for it, Joe, because this is going down,' I replied. I couldn't understand why the bank would not face reality. The property market had crashed and so had all their clients. In summing up the court case with Hugh McGivern, Justice Kelly had made reference to a rush to judgment by our creditors. This amounted to an invitation to other creditors to take action against us. He was helping us over the edge. That was the scenario Anglo were most worried about. An orderly cash-flow plan was something they could control, but third-party creditors and banks trying to take charges over our Anglo assets was not in their game plan. Things were accelerating and slipping outside their control.

After at least a year of planning for scenarios like this, the bank was far from ready. They were only now learning what to do when borrowers could not repay their loans. The lawyers we were all using were very sketchy on the applications of the Bankruptcy Act, because very few had ever used it. Theory books from college days were being dusted off and reread.

'It's a Victorian law that is not appropriate for today's world,' Aidan Marsh said to me, at one of our strategy meetings. Aidan was a partner with Beauchamps solicitors. He was the main solicitor in our commercial-property portfolio, and also a trusted, loyal friend. 'It was designed for English gentlemen who couldn't pay their gambling debts, not interconnected property developers owning hundreds of millions.' That summed it up. We were still relying on the bankruptcy laws that the British had left us with, which had not been updated as the world had modernized. The 1988 Act was a rehash of a piece of legislation from a different era.

Our advisers in the process were Kieran Ryan on the accountancy side and Beauchamps solicitors on the legal side. Paddy and I had worked on the last scheme of arrangement that had been undertaken in Ireland in the late 1990s. That was for Eddie Kavanagh and his brothers and it had been successful. The Kavanaghs were in the agri-food sector and their business had failed due to excessive bank debt and a collapse in food prices. Their numbers were much smaller than ours, but the principle was the same. Banks were pursuing them because they had given personal guarantees and they needed court protection.

Nobody was sure how a scheme of arrangement might play out, or how the bank would react. As developers we were now political cannon fodder and I was worried that this might interfere with the court process. The public had an appetite for blood and I did not want to be the one providing it.

Under a scheme of arrangement, you have to hold a series of creditors' meetings at which your creditors get to vote on your fate. If three-fifths of your creditors, by value and number, vote for the scheme, it is approved and you are free. In that scenario all your assets are repossessed or sold and your debts forgiven. It would be a completely clean start with no carryover from the past. This was an intoxicating prospect for me. If your creditors do not vote for a scheme, bankruptcy is the outcome.

On the morning of the meeting with the bank, I drove to Dublin early to meet with Chris. It was a beautiful late-spring day and the sun was beating down. The drive seemed to take longer than usual, and I turned on the radio to fill the time. The airwaves were filled with reports of the demise of the Celtic Tiger. Things were going to get very rough.

We had agreed to gather at Kieran Ryan's office an hour before the meeting so that we could walk up to the bank together. There, we went over the strategy for the meeting. We had had this conversation many times over recent months, but this was now for real. We had tossed the merits of a scheme of arrangement back and forth for at least a year, but this was it. We were insolvent and we were now operating without the support of our main bank. That left us open to attacks from other creditors and banks, and we had to be able to defend ourselves.

As we walked up to the bank, the conversation was light. It was up to the bank to make the running during the meeting, and suggest alternative options that might divert us from our planned course of action.

Debbie, who was Joe's personal assistant, came down to collect us, and we were brought into a small meeting room. The team from the bank were waiting for us. We had agreed to leave the lawyers behind for this meeting, but that did not mean the room was short of people. Their faces showed the stress of the past few days. Less than a week had passed since our day in court, but in that time, everything had changed. They say that bankruptcy happens very slowly at first, and then very fast. That was certainly how it was working out for us.

After a brief silence, Tony Carey opened the discussion on behalf of the bank. 'Why did you have to make that statement, Simon? It's caused a lot of problems for the bank,' he said, reiterating our previous conversation.

'It was the truth, Tony. We wanted to be honest with the court,' I said. We had known it would cause controversy, but we hadn't expected it to force Anglo into such a defensive position. It was meant to be a statement of truth rather than a weapon to damage the bank, but they did not see it like that.

'What are you looking for?' Tony asked. 'A payout of a hundred million euro?' That took me by surprise. I tried to work out whether he was offering me real money, or accusing me of blackmail. I think it was an offer, although clearly the figure was for effect. Was the bank really willing to pay us to go away?

'We're not here to extract anything, Tony. We want to see if there's a middle ground,' I answered, trying to defuse the situation.

We went on to explain our desire to find a solution that did not cause a problem for the bank. The bank was very concerned about the next sitting of the bankruptcy court on the following Monday. They were convinced that we were primed and ready to go at any moment. The truth was a little different. We had the numbers prepared but we had yet to brief a barrister, and we were certainly three or four weeks away from any court action. I was happy to leave the bank with the fear that action was pending, and I did nothing to alter their view on that.

The upshot of the meeting was a temporary ceasefire. We agreed to stay away from the courts, and they agreed to do nothing regarding receivers. The meeting broke up and we walked out into the sunshine. Despite the apparent peace, it was clear to me that they could turn on us at any moment. Any loyalty they once had was gone, and the bank would now do whatever was required to defend itself. Should I blame them for this? Probably not, but I felt a sense of loss and betrayal.

With the stand-down agreed, I got to work finalizing the scheme of arrangement. We might not need it, but I wanted it ready. I made the phone calls and we arranged our first round-table meeting with the barristers to take place as soon as possible at the offices of Beauchamps solicitors.

The team convened on 7 April, filling Beauchamps' boardroom. Anglo's unfinished new headquarters on the north docks again dominated the view – it seemed to provide a fitting backdrop to all my meetings in Beauchamps at that stage in the crisis. We had senior and junior counsel at the meeting. Most of my questions related to the effects of a scheme of arrangement on our partners and the underlying assets. We wanted to be able to pass away quietly as a business without taking anybody else with us.

The discussion was lively. We could go into the court on any given Monday and seek court protection and it would be granted. There was no doubt that we qualified for court protection, which would mean that no bank or creditor could take any action against us until the scheme was approved or voted down. This process would probably take up to two years.

The major down-side would be the legal costs – the whole process happens through the court system and that is a recipe for a very large legal bill. Even so, I was keen to move forward. I had been through the examinership process with Thomas Read's, and a lot of the concepts were the same. The open-ended nature of a private scheme looked very attractive to me when set against the hard 100-day limit of examinerships.

My first action after the meeting was to finalize our state-ment of assets and liabilities for the court. For the next three days I camped in Beauchamps with a solicitor and an account-ant and we verified every asset, its ownership and the level of debt. Those three days were like a final run down Memory Lane. The deals felt like pets to me, or sheep in a flock, and each one had its own importance. I wanted to be rid of them all, that was never in doubt, but I also wanted them to know that I remembered them. It was just time to move on and I hoped that their new owner would treat them well.

The written opinion from the barristers arrived in an email and it answered a number of our key queries and concerns.

The advice was long and complex but the message was simple. If we sought the court's protection, we would receive it, but the fallout would be considerable. There was no guarantee about the effect it might have on our partners, and that caused me the most concern. Most of our partners still believed that they were going to survive the crash. I held a different view, but I did not want to be the one to bring down the whole structure and drag them into the vortex.

I had built the bomb, in the form of a scheme of arrangement, but I was not willing to use it. I hoped that merely having it ready would be enough. I called the bank, and we decided to meet again. They, too, had been busy in the days following the meeting. They were trying to work out where they stood legally on every loan. If they had to act, what were their options? Their sole real weapon was receivership, but they could only use it against the entire property attached to a loan: there was no way to isolate an individual within a partnership. I think their feelings on this were similar to mine: they did not want to take everybody down. We both had the bomb now and both pulled back from the brink.

Now that we had decided not to fight, or defend, all that was left was to find a way to move on quietly. We wanted to avoid the fireworks and the associated drama of a lengthy court battle.

In the following weeks we worked with Anglo's solicitors and designed a way for our assets to be protected from third-party creditors and other banks. In all but name, our Anglo assets were now the property of the bank. We achieved that with an arrangement whereby we cross-secured our €70 million equity facility against all our other Anglo debts. This meant that Anglo would need to be fully paid before any other bank could get access to the equity we might have in a building. We had a number of uncharged shares in companies and Anglo made a grab for some of these to improve their position. Our power was gone the moment the bank saw we were not willing to go into a scheme. This left them the carcass of our business to pick over.

As I was moving on, the bank needed to know that somebody was going to manage the assets. We agreed on Robert Keogh, an Anglo banker who had become a developer and was in partnership with us on a number of deals. The team from Newlan Construction, his development company, formed a new company, which was specifically set up to manage some of our Anglo assets. The bank could not be seen to be making direct decisions on our behalf, so we had to have a number of masks to hide them. They agreed to pay the overheads and salaries of our reduced office and that was of central importance to me. I was happy to move on and face the world, but I wanted to leave some legacy and hope for the small team in the office. My brother Chris was part of this team, and he would become the new face of the Kellys in Anglo. Tony Carey's role was finished and the new structure limped onwards. All the changes and agreements meant nothing when it came to cash and virtually all expenditure was frozen. Projects were frozen, too, and nothing was to be done. We were to wait for NAMA and its great plan.

NAMA to me seemed like a good solution to a very bad problem. The banks had a lot of toxic property assets, and they were punch-drunk from the crash. A bank's standard answer to all queries now was 'no', even if what was being proposed was beneficial to it. I hoped that NAMA might breathe some new energy into the handling of toxic assets.

Once Anglo had their security they felt immune from the other banks. Before it had been put in place, the bank had had an incentive to work with us and keep us afloat. Now we were on our own.

The other banks moved in to take what they could. Bank of Ireland Private was first. They had also provided a flexible overdraft to the business in the good days, hoping for a juicy loan in return. They had never got it – they only ever made one small loan to us. Now, by litigating against Paddy and the business, they were hoping Anglo would step up and pay off their debt. They made that goal explicit during a meeting Paddy had with them to discuss the situation in April. With Anglo satisfied, we settled on a general strategy for the legal cases that were sure to follow. There was no point in fighting so we decided to consent to virtually all applications.

Judgments were like the personal guarantees we had signed to borrow the money from banks: once you signed the first big one, you might as well sign them all. The damaging one was the first, and after that, it was merely paper upon paper. I viewed the imposition of a court judgment as a confirmation of the fact that we were bust and nothing more than that.

Judgments allow their holders to follow a number of courses of action to try to claim their money. With the property market on the floor and frozen, none of these actions would provide any relief for the creditor. The legal actions generally stopped at a judgment and many of these were not even registered. They would pile up and wait for action in the distant future. Nothing could happen now. The banks soon tired of paying legal fees in return for more judgments. They realized they were throwing good money after bad.

The end was filled with silences, long, wonderful silences that I could wallow in after years of frenetic activity. Some days, I would not even bring my phone with me when I left the house. It no longer owned me. My email went quiet; I checked it only now and again. The urgency was gone.

There was nothing to be urgent about because there was nothing to save.

When I was immersed in the business I could not see it for what it was. Now it became clear to me. It had become a sad business full of sad people, running on treadmills to nowhere. Very little was created during the property boom. Corners were cut and shortcuts were always taken. There was no connectivity of thinking. In the end our island thinking sold us all short, leaving us fighting over scraps of earth that nobody else would care about.

The end brought relief from all of that and more. I was happy to bid it goodbye.

10. The Future

The boom was like a Ponzi scheme. It sucked in more and more people, and this went on for years. In the end a point was reached where there were no new people and no new money, and the collapse was the inevitable conclusion. The prospect of soft landings was always the talk of dreamers. For those who had the foresight to stay away and avoid the whole collapse, I'm jealous of your foresight.

I can understand how we did not see the madness of the bubble. This is the nature of bubbles: the participants cannot see what would be obvious to an external observer. I cannot remember a single instance during twenty years in the business when I encountered a foreign investor in the Irish property market. We built it by ourselves, and the collapse was because of us.

By the mid-2000s all of the cash in Ireland had already been sucked into the bubble. The bubble would have burst at that point except for the availability of seemingly unlimited funds through the interbank market. The Irish banks happily borrowed hundreds of billions from it and loaned them into the Irish property market, driving it higher. While it was going on, unlimited funds seemed to be available and we never saw any reason to believe that it would ever be otherwise. This was part of our self-delusion as developers. We were focused on the micro details and this caused us to miss the giant elephant in the room: the bubble and how it was being funded. These bank debts are now part of the Irish government's debt. In years to come, we may be grateful for the global credit crunch and the Lehman Brothers collapse: it probably saved us from an even bigger bubble.

The bursting of the bubble was traumatic, but it needed to happen. Hopefully we did not go too far, and destroy the whole country. Only time will tell.

The cheerleaders of the boom have been replaced by the legions of people who claim to have 'told you so'. This, too, is a common feature of bubbles and economics. It is referred to as 'hindsight bias'. I have tried to subdue this natural inclination in writing my book. I have tried to capture the emotions I experienced at the time, rather than change them to reflect my current feelings. If I'd known then what I know now . . .

On Wednesday, 2 September 2009, at ten thirty-two a.m., I opened my MacBook Pro and loaded Microsoft Word. I created a new file, which I called 'Lessons from the Boom'. Staring at the black screen, and sitting at my kitchen table, I began to document my thoughts. I had never done such a thing before. As a developer, I'd thought I was always right. Sitting down now, I was going to attempt to clarify where I'd gone wrong. I wanted to learn from my mistakes. I wanted to record my thoughts so that I could refer back to them in the future, when I was part of another booming business cycle.

As I tapped away at the keyboard, I had no idea that these lessons would ever become public. They were private thoughts for my own record. Now that I have written this book, it seems to me that they should form part of it. Was I destined to remain a mindless property developer, or could I learn and change? I was committed to learning from the boom and the bust, and this was to be my first crude effort.

Lessons from the Boom 1995–2009
by Simon Kelly
2 September 2009

1. Property is the same as any other asset. It is NOT special
*It has no magic properties and it can rise and fall as easily as other
assets. The lack of liquidity in the property markets tends to lengthen
the cycles on the up-side and the down-side, and this causes greater
booms and busts.*

    *The key driver for the value of property (and therefore its class as an
asset) is credit and its availability. Where credit is available, property
will flourish, and where credit is withdrawn, property will crash. The
owner of the debt on a property is the true owner and the risk on
property equity is much higher than people anticipate.*

    *'Buy and hold' as a principle has been dealt a terminal blow by this
credit crunch. 'Buy and trade' needs to be the new mantra if you are to
participate in the property market. The day you buy is the day you
sell. This means that the saleability of a property needs to be considered
prior to its purchase. Risky property such as resorts (which naturally
show high profit margins) are illiquid and dangerous to hold because
selling will be an issue. Don't buy something if you are not sure that
you can sell it again easily.*

    *Well-located modern capital cities offer the most liquid markets, and
are therefore the safest areas in which to invest. Returns on this style of
investment are low for this reason. Private equity will not generate a
sufficient return over the long term because it is competing with
pension-fund investors seeking 6–10 per cent.*

    *Commercial property is currently cheap and prices are still falling.
It will probably boom again. It is always worth looking to invest in
bubbles and growth markets at an early stage but the risks need to be
known and remembered. Over the long term, property is a low-return
inflation hedge and not a value-add investment. 'Buy and hold' is
dead, and early bubble buying makes sense.*

In summary, property is good as a low-return pension investment, good as an asset from which to draw an income from fees, and dangerous for speculation due to timeline to exit. Selling can be a problem.

The safest way to play a property bubble is by investing in listed shares of property companies, industry providers and banks. Sell well before the top, average in and average out. DO NOT BELIEVE THE HYPE AND NEW-PARADIGM-SPEAK.
For example, a property boom in Israel or Canada will lead to a bank boom. All markets will suffer distress over the long term. Nowhere is totally safe.

2. Profit is Profit
Profit net of tax is the only figure to value when looking at a business.
EBITDA (Earnings Before Interest, Tax, Depreciation and Amortization) is not profit and cash flow is not profit, despite what people may tell you.

Value is derived from profit, not turnover. Turnover is vanity. Profit is sanity.

3. Leverage – Friend or Foe?
The goal at the end of a business cycle needs to be unleveraged assets and cash.

In playing the bubbles of the market, leverage is your friend and should be used on a non-recourse basis. Well before the end of the bubble, leverage needs to be removed and all non-liquid assets disposed of. This is the theory of market timing. History is full of failures from people who attempted this. It must still be tried.

4. Don't Own What You Can't Manage
Do not own assets that you cannot manage or step in to run unless they have sufficient scale to merit professional management. As a trading asset fails, management will try to take over or jump ship leaving you

with a company that you need to manage but cannot. Loyalty will be forgotten by the actions of management motivated by self-preservation.

5. Make the world your marketplace

Ireland is a very pleasant place but it is not the only place and it should not be the centre of a business that has ambition to grow. Ireland is a small open economy that is exposed to the vagaries of the world market. This can be both positive and negative. The world is large and there are endless opportunities in both property and other businesses. Make this your market and enjoy Ireland for its other features.

6. Invest more money in fewer projects. Back your winners

As I analysed my statement of affairs during the crash, many of the projects seemed alien to me. I was merely a name on the project, or a contact for the bank. Only work on projects that you have passion for. Do not spread your valuable time over multiple projects offering very little to each one. Focus and deliver. Profits will follow.

7. Never Trust the Bank

This one is a little sad for me but certainly true. I am sure it will be challenged in the future. The actions of the banks in this crash were a disgrace as they strove to pass the blame on for bad lending practices. As per Lesson 1, property values are a derivative of bank liquidity and confidence. When both are removed by the banking system, it is illogical for banks to seek to blame others. The reliance on personal guarantees for almost all lending was one of the problems in Ireland during the boom. Banks seemed to rely on the myth of personality and followed this reliance with lots of credit. Had bankers attempted to analyse the actual projects they were financing, I think that a lot less debt would have been issued, with fewer personal legal actions following this debt. There is no logic in providing personal guarantees to banks. Raise sufficient capital for projects to operate without personal recourse. This will lower the

return on individual projects, but it will greatly enhance the
long-term sustainability of the business.

8. Watch Out For Bubbles
Bubbles are common and you will encounter many more in the future.
If something seems too good to be true, like the Irish property market,
it probably is.

9. Choose and Structure Partnerships Carefully
Partnership can allow you access to projects that would otherwise be too
large. In considering this benefit, the down-side of partnership must
also be measured. Partnership should start with friendship, because
this will survive most disputes. Dysfunctional partnerships should be
immediately ceased and the assets sold on the open market.

10. Always Have a Plan B
However smart and clever Plan A looks and performs for a number of
years, have Plan B at the ready. The future is different from the past
so you cannot trust it. A backup plan that is real and tested validates
and protects you from this unknown future.

During the entire boom, I never met a property person who did not believe in the validity of the market and its prices. Everything was anchored on seemingly concrete prices, which turned out to be built on sand. The commentators from the sidelines did not have the credibility to challenge the prevailing market, so their views were ignored. No real debate was allowed to take place, and in the absence of this debate, the status quo prevailed – 'The boom got boomier', as Bertie put it.

The one commentator who struck a chord with me was David McWilliams. I used to drive to Dublin daily and listen to his view on the market blaring out of the radio. I did not like the message at the time, but I did not change the channel. Despite his constant challenging of the market, and my inside knowledge, it took me years to challenge the market in my thinking; and even when I did finally come around, I lacked the strength to push through the sales and leave the game. This seems to be a common factor for all developers. We stayed at the table gambling with each other until the casino burned down around us.

The overriding lesson that everybody can take from this period of Irish history is the need constantly and vigorously to challenge the prevailing view. When everybody is going up the road, it's time to walk down it. Contrarian thinking and investing is difficult: to step out from the crowd and do something different is to feel alone, and that is not a natural human inclination. The comfort is in the crowd, even if it's heading over a cliff. But if you challenge the concepts behind everything, you'll lessen your chance of failure.

Property was the rock on which Irish society was built, and economic life seemed to revolve around it. This is, at least in part, a consequence of our previous existence as landless tenant farmers. To own land was to live and survive, so the importance of ownership has been drilled into our minds. A distortion created by the bubble was the social insecurity inflicted on people who did not own property. To live a tenant's life was to be stricken with an illness in the eyes of others. Society's cure for this illness was mortgage approval, based on a boosted income statement. Everything on the mortgage application was maxed out so your loan could be maxed out. The net result of this process was an overpriced house or apartment, but a warm feeling inside. Now home ownership has been exposed as the serious financial risk that it is.

When I started in property development with my father in the 1980s, it was a small business with just a few participants. The UK was our market, because there was no demand in Ireland. With the oversupply now clear for all to see, a similar period of quiet will fall on the property business in Ireland.

As the business grew in the 1990s and boomed in the 2000s, the number of people involved grew at a similar rate. I built a large office team and surrounded myself with outsourced services, and so did many other developers. Law firms expanded to handle the volume of transactions, and the banks grew to an enormous size. These are only the obvious parts of the business. The government payroll was fattened with the tax receipts from the property boom. Immigrants came to Ireland to work on the sites.

The property industry is now being dismantled and downsized, and this adjustment will continue to feed through the whole economy. The shift away from property will be partially offset by the creation of new businesses and prospects. This will clearly take longer than the rapid destruction of the property side of the economy, and the intervening years of pain will seem endless to some. The property boom gave the country a false prosperity, and its crash will continue to cause considerable distress and social unrest. This can only be offset and mitigated by the creation of new businesses, and this is the transformation we need to seek.

As the crash accelerated, I kept asking myself, 'What will all the people do?'

The answer to this has become clearer as time has passed. We now know that many will stay and operate on a lower level of income. The solicitors and accountants who profited from the boom are in this category. Some will stay and wait for the market to start again. In this category, we see the swelling dole queues full of construction workers. Many will leave the country seeking work in more productive climates like Canada and Australia. Emigration causes outcries from the media, but it is a positive move. For Ireland to develop to its full potential, we will need people who have been externally trained in business and life. Their experiences in the wider world can only benefit Ireland when they come home, as many will.

The remaining few will change what they do, and this is the group I am most interested in. Those who stand up and try something new, having taken the knocks of the crash, will generate a new energy for Ireland. This is the group that I want to be part of. New energy will generate new income and this is the healing force that will fix our balance-sheet problems.

The property business in the boom was a very personal and individualistic business. The bust has been similarly personal, and most developers are insolvent due to the guarantees they signed.

The business will be very different in the future and it will be structured in a corporate environment. I doubt that anybody with the experience from this bust will ever trade personally again. The risk is clearly too high.

The syndicated nature of the RQB model is a potential future for property development. More equity and less debt should be used, and the only real route to this kind of equity is through syndication. People will need to club together around some central management to get projects under way. The need for projects is still some time off into the future, because of the excess of supply, but demand will come back. Buildings disintegrate, and go out of date, and new buildings will always be needed.

Property will be seen as a utility asset and inflation hedge, not a one-way bet. Expected returns will more closely follow growth and inflation over the coming years. In similar crashes in other countries, property underperformed inflation for many years afterwards. I think that this will be avoided in Ireland, because of our deep attachment to property. Despite the fortunes that have been lost and wasted, many people will view property as a recovery play on Ireland. Buying will speed up once a solid bottom is reached and the graph for property will again point upwards.

A lot of our imagined wealth was tied up in property, and in the future this wealth will be spread among a number of other assets. I think we will all have more cash in relation to our borrowings and we will also have assets overseas. The sight of pensioners at bank AGMs, ruined by the crash, will stay long in our minds when it comes to saving for retirement. I do not think that the banks will again be trusted with such responsibility.

The property business that remains in place after the crash will look a lot more like a service industry than the commercial monster I was part of. NAMA is now the largest land and building owner in Ireland, which relegates all other participants to the status of service providers. NAMA will have access to funding at far superior rates to the private sector, so I see little point in trying to compete with it as a property owner. It will be like a blue whale swimming through the Irish Sea. Small fish will surround the giant to feed off its scraps.

A lot has been written about NAMA, its rights and wrongs. In the end I think it is probably the right solution for the Irish bubble. NAMA allowed the government to play for time, and making the process slow has allowed it to extend this time. This is the tribunal approach to solving problems and it seems to be an Irish favourite: it pushes issues out over the long term, and on this kind of timeline new solutions appear, which were not initially available.

As I write, I have not yet met with NAMA, which is currently digesting the top ten developers. (Redquartz did not quite make this league, for which I have to be thankful.) The people running NAMA seem to realize that nothing can be achieved until the acute stage of the crisis has passed, and therefore there is no rush. Symbolically, bankrupting developers would offer little in the way of solutions: it would merely serve to satisfy the public appetite for blood, and enrich the solicitors who work in the bankruptcy court. This does not seem to be a path they will choose.

At the beginning of 2010 I started writing a column for the *Sunday Tribune*. In my opening piece I said I was sorry for the 'long-term fiscal damage' that I, and others in the property business, had done to Ireland. That was true then and it's still true now. The property market is large and complex, and the actions of an individual cannot change its course. If I had never participated in the industry, the result would have been the same. But I was a willing participant so I am partially responsible for what happened.

My instincts told me that something was wrong with the property business, but I did not act on this with sufficient conviction. I am now a stricken developer as a result of this inaction. I have never tried to hide from this fact. The past is now history, but its lessons will stay with me for ever.

Index